DEPRESSION, SUBJECTIVE WELL-BEING AND INDIVIDUAL ASPIRATIONS OF COLLEGE STUDENTS

Depression, Subjective Well-Being and Individual Aspirations of College Students

Ferenc Margitics

and

Zsuzsa Pauwlik

Nova Science Publishers, Inc.

New York

NOTICE TO THE READER

The Publisher has taken reasonable care in the preparation of this book, but makes no expressed or implied warranty of any kind and assumes no responsibility for any errors or omissions. No liability is assumed for incidental or consequential damages in connection with or arising out of information contained in this book. The Publisher shall not be liable for any special, consequential, or exemplary damages resulting, in whole or in part, from the readers' use of, or reliance upon, this material.

Independent verification should be sought for any data, advice or recommendations contained in this book. In addition, no responsibility is assumed by the publisher for any injury and/or damage to persons or property arising from any methods, products, instructions, ideas or otherwise contained in this publication.

This publication is designed to provide accurate and authoritative information with regard to the subject matter covered herein. It is sold with the clear understanding that the Publisher is not engaged in rendering legal or any other professional services. If legal or any other expert assistance is required, the services of a competent person should be sought. FROM A DECLARATION OF PARTICIPANTS JOINTLY ADOPTED BY A COMMITTEE OF THE AMERICAN BAR ASSOCIATION AND A COMMITTEE OF PUBLISHERS.

LIBRARY OF CONGRESS CATALOGING-IN-PUBLICATION DATA

Margitics, Ferenc.
 Depression, subjective well-being, and individual aspirations of college students / Authors, Ferenc Margitics and Zsuzsa Pauwlik.
  p. cm.
 Includes index.
 ISBN 978-1-60692-851-6 (softcover)
 1. Depression in adolescence. 2. College students--Mental health. I. Pauwlik, Zsuzsa. II. Title.
 RJ506.D4M285 2009
 616.85'2700835--dc22
                    2008050306

Published by Nova Science Publishers, Inc. ✦ New York

CONTENTS

PREFACE

Health psychology – a branch of psychology with a brief three decades of history – appeared in Hungary in the late 1990s and has become an organic part of local psychology studies in recent years.

Health psychology courses are now organic parts of both the BA and the MA programs, and specialised psychologist training courses. Health psychologist training was launched in 2007 in Hungary.

Health psychology courses were introduced at several universities in the country and there are many research groups that undertake studies in health psychology. In order to improve communication and collaboration among the research groups and the training institutions, and to promote health psychological awareness in a broader context, a conference titled *"Egészségpszichológia Magyarországon: Oktatás, kutatás, együttműködés" [Health Psychology In Hungary: Education, Research, Collaboration]* was organised in Budapest on 23 April, 2004, and was followed by other similar events.

The College of Nyíregyháza's Department of Psychology, within the Faculty of Education, formed its Health Psychology Group in 2005. The College of Nyíregyháza (www.nyf.hu) operates in the Eastern region of Hungary, in Nyíregyáza, a county seat of 120,000 inhabitants. Presently there are five faculties at the college (Arts, Economics and Social Studies, Science, Engineering and Agriculture, Education) which run 24 BA and BSc courses. There are more than 12,000 students pursuing studies at the college.

The major research areas of the Health Psychology Group are the following:

- The background factors of coping with depressive experiences (2005-2006)
- The connections between individual aspirations and religiousness/spirituality, and subjective well-being and emotional intelligence (2007-2008)

It is hoped that the results of this research can contribute to the effectiveness of prevention programmes which deal with the mental health of young people, and, furthermore, provide information for the work of those professionals who specialise in young adults.

The Health Psychology group launched a research project in 2005 which focussed on the study of the subclinical depression syndrome. The subclinical depression syndrome refers to an emotionally negative state which significantly influences level of achievement and quality of life, but which cannot yet be classified as an illness. Based on the seriousness of the symptoms, it could be measured on different scales of depression as mild or moderate.

One of the aims of the research was to find out what characterizes the state of mind of college students, whether the hopelessness, despondency and subclinical depressive mood, nationally found among Hungarian citizens, are also typical of them. The other aim of the research was to examine and discover in their complexity those factors which have a role in the development of subclinical depression syndrome.

In this book the findings of our research performed hitherto in the mentioned fields are presented.

Chapter 1 - In the course of our study we seek an assessment of the mental state of today's college students; to what extent can subclinical depression syndrome be detected in this circle. Analyses were carried out in two phases, in 2004 and in 2007. In 2004, 681 students (465 women, 216 men), in 2007, 712 students (545 women, 167 men) took part in the analysis. A short 13-item screening scale of the Beck Depression Inventory was used in the analyses. Our research demonstrates that the occurrence of subclinical depression syndrome in college student populations displayed higher proportions than what has been found in representative assessment in populations above 16 years. Our research emphasizes that more than half of college students suffer from a feeling of worthlessness and discontentment. Besides almost every second college student could be characterized as exhausted, undecided and hopeless. The tendency occurred regardless of sex, however in cases of females proportions of occurrences appeared less superior than in cases of males. Our research data show that the result displays not only a temporary state of mind of our college youth, but an enduring – at least for four years – situation.

Chapter 2 - In the course of our research, efforts have been made to find out whether predispositional factors are present in healthy college students who have a successful socialization and are able to show socially accepted and acknowledged performance. Out of the individuals involved in the survey (n=681), 465 were men and 216 were women. The research group consisted of students with any of the predispositional factors: positive family anamnesis (mother's, father's, sibling's or grandparent's depression), loss (death of parent, separation, parents' divorce during the first ten years of the child). The control group consisted of students with none of the predispositional factors. The distribution of the individuals taking part in the research was the following: 232 persons (161 women and 71 men) in the research group and 219 (135 women and 84 men) in the control group. Our findings illustrate that the predispositional factors relevant to the inclination to depression are also effective in non-clinical populations. In addition to this, we have demonstrated that certain family socializational effects may also function as predispositional factors.

Chapter 3 - In the course of our research we were seeking an answer to what backgrounds are in close interrelation with the sub-clinical depressive syndromes in college students, whose socialization can be considered successful, and who belong to the non-clinical population. We examined the following background factors: temperament and character features of personality, the dysfunctional attitudes, the coping strategies, the attributional style, as well as the factors of individual family socialization. 681 college students were involved in the research (465 women, and 216 men students). The results of our research show that the lack of effective coping, some jeopardising factors of family socialisation, some attitudes becoming dysfunctional, and the passive attribution style have the closest interrelation with the depressive syndrome.

Chapter 4 - The aim of this research was to discover in a group of young, and healthy people (college students) not belonging to the clinical population the risk and protective factors having a role in the development of predisposition to depression and being related to family socialisation factors. The sample was taken on the basis of the existence or lack of predisposing factors (positive family anamnesis to depression, death of parents, separation and divorce in the first ten years of the child's life): 232 persons belonged to the group of imperilled people (161 women, 71 men), and 219 persons were in the control group (135 women, 84 men). The group of imperilled persons were further divided on the basis of the results achieved in Beck's Depression Inventory (BDI) for a group of normal level (n=104, 63 women, 41 men) and a high level depression (n=128, 98 women, 30 men) group. For the examination of the family socialisation effects we used Goch's Family Socialisation Inquiry, and the Hungarian adaptation of the Parental Treatment Inquiry developed by Parker et al. On grounds of a non-clinical sample our survey substantiated that certain family socialisation factors may also play a role as risk and protective factors in the development of depression particularly in the case of vulnerable persons. We managed to substantiate that the primary risk factors were the punishing and neglecting way of breeding by parents, the manipulative, inconsistent and consistent educational attitudes, the conflict-filled family attitude, and several elements of parental treatment (restraint, lack of affection and care, intensified overprotection). We managed to indicate as a protective factor the defending effect, principally, of the supportive and less punishing educational style of parents, the lack of manipulative and inconsistent educational attitude, the tranquil family atmosphere, the homogeneous parental breeding, as well as the paternal treatment showing affection, care, restrictions but less over-protection.

Chapter 5 - Our research aimed to find out what role the risk mechanisms, as described in Goodman and Gotlib's (1999) model (genetic-biological, interpersonal, social learning related cognitive and stress related factors), play in the development of increased risk for depression in the case of men and women. The genetic-biological factors were examined with certain temperament characteristics, the interpersonal factors with parental educational purpose, educational attitudes, educational style and parental treatment. In the case of factors related to social learning we looked at the dysfunctional attitudes and the attributional style. As far as the stressors are concerned, we observed the quality of family atmosphere, and the number of the positive and negative life events of the preceding six months and their subjective evaluation. 681 students took part in the research (465 women and 216 men). Our research results show that all of the increased risk mechanisms, namely the genetic-biological, interpersonal, social learning related cognitive, and stress related factors are connected with the development of liability to depression, explaining 41.4% of the depression symptoms' variance in the case of women, and 36.5% in the case of men. Harm avoidance, a genetic-biological factor, proved to be the most significant risk mechanism, irrespective of the sexes. From among the environmental factors – irrespective of the sexes - one stress related factor, the subjective evaluation of negative life experiences, which implies an increased sensitivity to stress, proved to be the strongest risk mechanism. While the above factors played an important role in the development of vulnerability to depression in both sexes, the social learning related cognitive and interpersonal risk mechanisms differed in their degree in women and men. In the case of women the social learning related mechanisms proved to be stronger and higher impact risk factors than in the case of men. The effect of interpersonal factors seemed to be relatively the weakest in the development of increased risk for depression.

Chapter 6 - The objective of this study is to scrutinize the interrelations of the temperament and character types that are separable well by means of the Cloninger's Temperament and Character Inventory (TCI) with the depressive syndromes, dysfunctional attitudes and coping strategies among college students. There were 465 women and 216 men students (n=681) involved in the research. The Temperament and Character Inventory was used for separating the temperament and character types while the abridged version of Beck's Depression Inventory was applied for measuring the rate of depression. The dysfunctional attitudes were determined by the usage of the Hungarian version of Weismann's Dysfunctional Attitude Scale, and the coping strategies were examined through the Hungarian adaptation of Folkman and Lazarus's Conflict Solving Questionnaire. The findings of the studies demonstrated that each temperament and character type could be typified with an individual combination of depressive syndroms, dysfunctional attitudes, and coping strategies. During our surveys we discovered the dysfunctional attitudes and coping strategies being typical of the mature and immature character types.

Chapter 7 - In the course of our research we examined the level of subjective well-being among college students, and what individual aspirations they had. There were 545 women and 167 men students (n=712) involved in the research. In terms of the indicators of subjective well-being, students scored the highest values in self-evaluation, followed by positive attitude to life and pleasures of life. The low values measured on the depressive scale suggest the lack of depressive moods. No considerable difference between the two genders was measured at subjective well-being. The only exemption to that was observed at somatic symptoms and reactions, as women were found to be more susceptible to such reactions than men. When examining the importance of individual aspirations, we recorded the highest points at health, personal progress and social connections. Most participants in the survey found these personal aspirations very important. The college students involved in the project ascribed the lowest importance to the three extrinsic aspirations: fame, wealth and image. Intrinsic aspirations were therefore favoured by college students over the extrinsic ones. If priorities are examined in a breakdown according to genders, intrinsic aspirations were found more important by both sexes, with slight differences in emphasis. In terms of the probability of various types of aspiration, the highest scores were also measured at intrinsic aspirations. In that case, the order ot priority was social relations, personal progress and health. It was followed by social commitment and, finally, extrinsic aspirations, in the order of image, wealth and fame. When the order of probability is examined in a breakdown according to genders, women fully comply with the general trend, whereas in the case of the men there is a slight deviation at one point only, they tend to place wealth before image. In terms of the implementation of the types of aspiration, the tendency is similar, as we find the highest points at the intrinsic ones, in the following order: social relations, health and personal progress. Here an extrinsic aspiration, image wedged in, followed by social commitment, wealth and fame. The order was the same for both sexes.

Chapter 1

SUBCLINICAL DEPRESSION SYNDROME AS A HEALTH CARE RISK FACTOR IN COLLEGE STUDENTS

ABSTRACT

In the course of our study we seek an assessment of the mental state of Hungarian college students; to what extent can subclinical depression syndrome be detected in this circle. Analyses were carried out in two phases, in 2004 and in 2007. In 2004: 681 students (465 women, 216 men), in 2007: 712 students (545 women, 167 men) took part in the analysis. A short 13-item screening scale of the Beck Depression Inventory was used in the analyses. Our research demonstrates that the occurrence of subclinical depression syndrome in college student populations displayed higher proportions than what has been found in representative assessment in populations above 16 years. Our research emphasizes that more than half of college students suffer from a feeling of worthlessness and discontentment. Besides almost every second college student could be characterized as exhausted, undecided and hopeless. The tendency occurred regardless of sex, however in cases of females, proportions of occurrences appeared less superior than in cases of males. Our research data show that the result displays not only a temporary state of mind of our college youth, but an enduring – at least for four years – situation.

1. INTRODUCTION

The results of psychiatric epidemiological research show that depression has become one of the most common illnesses of our time. Based on Hungarian and international data, nearly 20 percent of adults have, at least once in their life, experienced a depressive episode and the prevalence of chronic depression is over 10 percent [1].

According to the results of research using self-rating scales, depressive syndrome is also very frequent in samples taken from the Hungarian population. 34% of women and 19% of men interviewed reported symptoms of depression, which in the case of women reached 11.8% whereas in the case of men 5.5 % of the serious clinical level [2,3]. The subclinical depression syndrome refers to an emotionally negative state which significantly influences level of achievement and quality of life, but which cannot be yet classified as an illness. Based on the seriousness of the symptoms, it could be measured on different scales of depression as mild or moderate [4].

International and domestic research programmes suggest that the worldwide prevalence of depression is around 7-15%. The research of Weissman et al., conducted in several countries, indicates the worldwide prevalence of unipolar depression has been on the increase since 1915, and the average age of when depression first occurs becomes younger and younger; at present it is 27 in the USA [5].

The occurence of depression increases among those who are at the age of 11 to 15 years. The occurence of depression episodes before the age of 18 is 15-20%, that of dystymia is 1.6-8%. [6].

The major biological and psycho-social changes in adolescents, as well as the altering social structures that bring about a much higher number of conflict situations, contribute to the increase of depression [7].

Kopp et al. [3] pointed out that all self-destructive forms of behaviour that today represent the highest general health risks emerge at that age. Such are smoking, alcohol problems, drug abuse, lifestyle poor in physical exercise and pathological eating habits.

Most young people are able to cope with the difficulties of adolescence successfully, without any permanent emotional damage. Students at colleges and universities, theoretically, belong to this category. They are faced with the problems of shaping their social identity. An important part of this process is the development of professional self-knowledge, improving their ability to match their chosen profession and professional identity. These issues may, naturally, also produce crisis situations for young people, and the solutions of these situations largely depend on the mental-hygienic state of the individual concerned [8].

Researchers dealing with behaviour-epidemiology pay relatively little attention to the college and university, as they tend to focus on more endangered risk groups and young people who suffer from mental illness.

Kopp and Skrabski [9] in the course of a survey of the psychic background of self-destructive behaviour of Hungarian university students in1989, found that the students lacked adequate objectives in life and strategies for coping with conflicts. All these may also lead to the emergence of subclinical depression syndromes in the students.

The objective of our research has been to find out how widespread the subclinical depression syndrome, what the general psychological situation of the Hungarian college students is, to what extent are they characterised by the hopelessness and depressive state of mind that is largely characteristic of the Hungarian population.

2. METHOD

Participants

Data gathering from the students of the College of Nyíregyháza took place in two phases, in 2004 and 2007. We collected data randomly from students of all the four faculties of the college. Participation was voluntary, with the explicit agreement of the students. The questionnaries were completed by the students at the lecture halls of the college, where the researchers were also present to offer assistance when needed.

As it has been referred to, the survey was conducted in two phases, in 2004 and 2007.

In 2004, 700 college students were involved in the survey. Out of them, 681 submitted an assessable questionnaire (465 women, 216 men). The distribution according to subject majors was the following: 225 studied to be teachers of art, 125 students studied science, 125 were students of economy, 74 studied to be infant teachers, 70 to be social studies teachers and 62 were students of music and graphic art. The average age was 19.98 (standard deviation: 1.51; min: 18, max 25), the value of the median was 20 years.

In 2007, 750 college students were involved in the survey. Out of them, 712 submitted an assessable questionnaire (545 women, 167 men). The distribution according to subject majors was the following: 165 studied to be teachers of art, 115 students studied science, 242 were students of economics, 77 were to be social studies teachers, 67 to be teachers of graphic art, and 46 of them studied to be infant teachers. The average age was 19.8 (standard deviation: 1.58; min: 18, max 27), the value of the median was 20 years.

Measures

To study depression we applied an abridged version of the 13 item multiple-choice questionnaire of the Beck Depression Inventory [10, 11]. The inventory studies the following components of depressive syndromes: sadness, pessimism, sense of failure, dissatisfaction, guilt, fear of punishment, suicide thoughts, indecisiveness, social withdrawal, self-image change, work difficulty, fatigability and anorexia.

The limits in the questionnaires are the following:

- 0-5 no depression
- 6-11 slight depression
- 12-15 medium depression
- 15 serious depression

3. RESULTS

The descriptive statistics of the results measured according to Beck's Depression Inventory for the whole pattern and in a breakdown according to the genders are provided below (M=mean value, SD=standard deviation).

Total:

- 2004: M=5.9; SD=4.2
- 2007: M=6.1; SD=5.4

Women:

- 2004: M=6.4; SD=4.4
- 2007: M=6.3; SD=5.2

Men:

- 2004: M=5; SD=3.7
- 2007: M=5.4; SD=5.9

A comparative statistical analysis of depression at the two genders (two-paired t-test) indicates that the depression level in females is significantly higher than that of men (2004: t=3.739, p<0.000; 2007: t=3.124, p<0.000).

The occurence of subclinical depression syndrome in the sample group was also examined. Figure 1 suggests that the occurence of depression syndrome was not considerably different among our college students from the figures found by Kopp et al. [2], although our figures were somewhat higher.

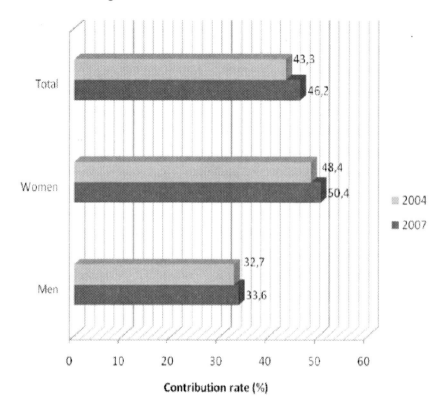

Figure 1. Occurrence of Subclinical Depressive Syndrome among college students.

According to Becker's [5] summary, more women tend to go through serious unipolar depression than men. This proportion is reflected by the results of Beck's survey conducted on a subclinical sample.

The occurrence of various depression symptoms (including varieties of mild and medium-seriousness as well) within the sample is shown in figure 2.

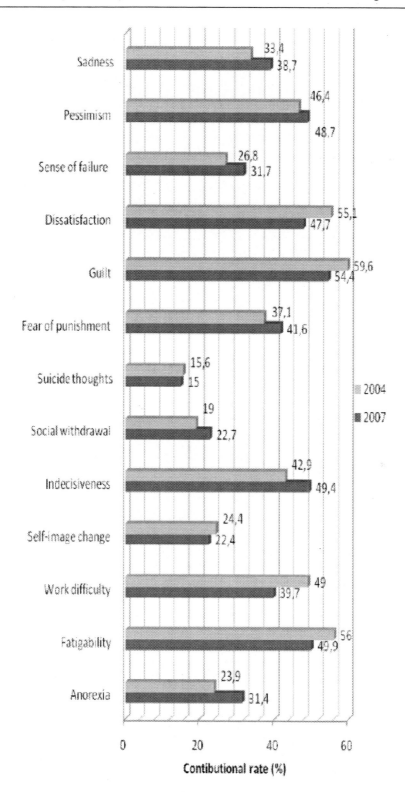

Figure 2. The occurrence rate of depressive syndromes in the complete sample as per Beck's Depression Inventory.

The data in the chart indicate that out of the various depression symptoms (varieties of mild and medium-seriousness) college students were primarily characterized by a sense of guilt (59.6%) in 2004. Work difficulty (56%) and dissatisfaction (55.1%) also occured at more than half of them. It was followed by a sense of inability to work (48%), pessimism (46.4%) and indecisiveness (42.9%). Out of all the symptoms, suicide thoughts (15.6%) and social withdrawal (19%) were of the lowest proportion.

In 2007, the most characteristic symptoms of depression among college students was guilt (54.4%). Almost half of them also complained of fatigability (49.9%), indecisiveness (49.4%), pessimism (48.7%) and dissatisfaction (47.7%). The occurance of suicidial thoughts was the lowest (15%).

It was also examined whether there was any difference between the two sexes (figures 3 and 4).

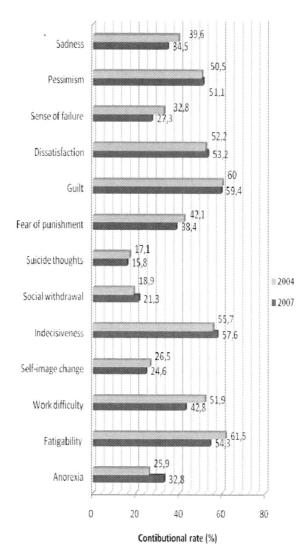

Figure 3. The occurrence rate of depressive syndrome in the case of women as per Beck's Depression Inventory.

In 2004, women were primarily characterised by fatigability (61.5%) and guilt (60%) of the symptons of depression. More than half of them complained of indecisiveness (55.7%), a sense of dissatisfaction (52.2%), work difficulty (51.9%), and pessimism (50.5%). Suicide thoughts and social withdrawal were the least frequent symptoms with 17,1% and 18,9% respectively. In 2007, the most common symptoms of depression among women were the following: a sense of guilt (59.4%) and indecisiveness (57.6%). More than half of the women in the group examined complained of fatigability (54.3%), dissatisfaction (53.2%), and pessimism (51.1%). Suicide thoughts (15.8%) and social withdrawal (21.3%) were the least common of all the depression symptoms.

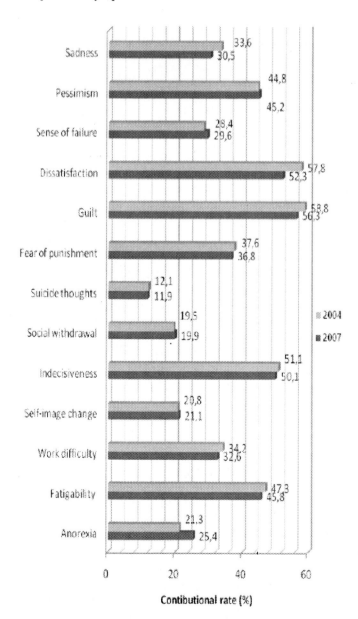

Figure 4. The occurrence rate of depressive syndrome in the case of men as per Beck's Depression Inventory.

As for the statistics for male students in 2004, male students were primarily affected by the following symptoms of depression: guilt (58.8%) and dissatisfaction (57.8%). More than half of them also complained of an indecisiveness (51.1%). Suicide thoughts and social withdrawal were the least common of the symptoms of depression with a prevalence of (12.1%) and (19.5%) respectively. In 2007, the symptoms of depression most common amond men were the following: guilt (56.3%) and dissatisfaction (52.3%). More than half of them also complained of an indecisiveness (50.1%). Suicide thoughts and social withdrawal were the least common of the symptoms of depression with a prevalence of (11.9%) and (19.9%) respectively.

A comparative statistical analysis of depression in the two sexes (two-paired t-test) indicates that the sense of pessimism (2004: $t=3.907$, $p<0,000$; 2007: $t=2.568$, $p<0.003$), fatigability (2004: $t=3.831$, $p<0.000$; 2007: $t=3.216$, $p<0.000$) and anorexia (2004: $t=3.809$, $p<0.000$; 2007: $t=3,753$, $p<0.000$) at women is significantly higher than they are in the case of men. Furthermore, women tend to have a more negative image of their own physical appearance than men (2004: $t=4.053$, $p<0.000$; 2007: $t=3.971$, $p<0.000$).

4. DISCUSSION

The findings of our research indicate that the prevalence of subclinical depression syndrome among college students is higher than what Kopp et al. [2,3] found as a result of their representative survey of the Hungarian population over 16 years of age.

According to our research, more than half of the college students suffer from guilt and dissatisfaction. Furthermore, almost every other college student was found to be characterised by fatigability, indecisiveness and pessimism. The tendency appears to be independent of sexes, although the prevalence of the symptoms is slightly higher in women than in men.

It is well reflected by our research findings that the results do not describe a mere temporary and transitory situation in the psychological situation of college youth in Hungary. It is a lasting situation that has existed for a minimum of four years.

If we analyse the subclinical depression symptom from the aspects of evolution psychology, they may be interpreted as distress signals through which college and university students express their loneliness and desperate efforts of trying to find a way out. In this way, our research findings are primarily useful for experts working in the field of mental hygiene and prevention at colleges and universities. The number of such experts is, regrettably, low at present. A large proportion of students in higher education therefore does not receive any support, they are alone with their problems, bad mood, sense of guilt and dissatisfaction, trying to use erroneous coping strategies to overcome the tensions caused by all this.

The research findings lead us to the conclusion that in the future greater emphasis should be placed upon developing the personality of university and college students and, within that, improving their self-esteem, and assisting them in developing adequate coping strategies. It is possible to incorporate mental-hygienic potentials and methods into the curricula of higher educational institutions in direct as well as indirect ways. A direct form is incorporating mental-hygienic skills in the contents of course materials. An indirect method may be the organization of career-socialization groups that function as an efficient mental-hygienic medium through developing the personality of students in a career-based way. Another indirect method is introducing ambulatory mental-hygienic services at university and college campuses.

REFERENCES

[1]   Kiss, H.G., & Szabó, A., & Rihmer, Z. (1998). A depresszió. Egy népbetegség korszerű megközelítése. [Depression. The modern approach of an endemic.] *Praxis, 7,* 7-13.

[2]   Kopp, M., & Szedmák, S., & Lőke, J., & Skrabski, Á. (1997). A depressziós tünetegyüttes gyakorisága és egészségügyi jelentősége a mai magyar lakosság körében. [The frequency and health importance of depression symptoms among the Hungarian population today.] *Lege Artis Medicine, 7,* 136-144.

[3]   Kopp, M., & Csoboth, CS., & Purebl, Gy. (1999). Fiatal nők egészségi állapota. [Young women's health status.] In: T. Pongrácz & I.Gy. Tóth (Eds.): *Szerepváltozások* (pp.239-259). Budapest: TÁRKI.

[4]   Margitics, F. (2006): *Depresszió. [Depression.]* Nyíregyháza: Krúdy Könyvkiadó.

[5]   Becker, J. (1989): *Depresszió. [Depression.]* Budapest: Gondolat.

[6]   Rudolph, K. D., Hammen, C. (1999). Age and gender as determinants of stress exposure, generation, and reactions in youngsters: A transactional perspective. *Child Development, 70,* 660-667.

[7]   Pikó B., & Fitzpatrick K. M. (2001): A rizikó és protektív elmélet alkalmazása a serdülőkori depressziós tünetegyüttes magatartás-epidemiológiai vizsgálatában. [Appllying the risk and protective factors approach to the behavioral epidemiological study of adolescent depression.] *Mentálhigiéné és Pszichoszomatika,* 41-47.

[8]   Bugán, A. (1999). Mentálhigiénés lehetőségek és módszerek a felsőoktatásban. [Facilities and methods in the mental hygienic in the higher education.] In E. Bagdy (Ed.), *Mentálhigiéné. Elmélet, gyakorlat, képzés, kutatás [Mental hygienic. Theory, practice, education, research.]* (pp.135-140). Budapest: Animula.

[9]   Kopp M., & Skrabski Á. (1995): *Alkalmazott magatartástudomány. [Applied behavioral science.]* Budapest: Corvinus Kiadó.

[10]   Beck, A.T., & Beck R.W. (1972). Screening depressed patients in family practice. A rapid technique. *Postgraduate Medicine, 52,* 81-85.

[11]   Margitics, F. (2005). Prediszponáló tényezők kapcsolata a szubklinikus depressziós tünetegyüttessel főiskolai hallgatóknál. [Interrelation between predisposition factors and sub clinical depression syndrome at college students.] *Psychiatria Hungarica, 20,* 211-223.

Chapter 2

THE APPLICABILITY OF THE VULNERABILITY THEORY AT THE EXAMINATION OF SUBCLINICAL DEPRESSION SYNDROME IN COLLEGE STUDENTS

ABSTRACT

In the course of our research, efforts have been made to find out whether predispositional factors are present in healthy college students who have a successful socialization and are able to show socially accepted and acknowledged performance. Out of the individuals involved in the survey (n=681), 465 were men and 216 were women. The research group consisted of students with any of the predispositional factors: positive family anamnesis (mother's, father's, sibling's or grandparent's depression), loss (death of parent, separation, parents' divorce during the first ten years of the child). The control group consisted of students with none of the predispositional factors. The distribution of the individuals taking part in the research was the following: 232 persons (161 women and 71 men) in the research group and 219 (135 women and 84 men) in the control group. Our findings illustrate that the predispositional factors relevant to the inclination to depression are also effective in non-clinical populations. In addition to this, we have demonstrated that certain family socializational effects may also function as predispositional factors.

1. INTRODUCTION

Surveys conducted with self-evaluation scales indicate that the occurrence of depression syndrome among the population is high. 18-34% of women and 10-19% of men report depression symptoms, reaching the serious clinical level at 6-11.8% of women and 2.6-5.5% of men [1].

Kopp et al. carried out a representative survey of the Hungarian population in 1995, and found that 31.8% of all the persons interviewed complained about symptoms of depression, 14% of them reported medium level, whereas 7% reported serious depression. Serious depression syndrome was found in 7.7% of women and 6.3% of the men [2].

An increase of the occurrence of depression syndrome takes place in the early adolescent ages, 11-15 years [3].

According to the vulnerability theory developed by Abramson, Brown and Harris, depression emerges as a result of an interaction of the human individual and their environment. An interaction of predispositional and provoking factors is required for the appearance of depression [4, 5, 6].

Brown and Harris assert that there are three basic psychosocial factors in the emergence of vulnerability [6]:

- The occurrence of the disorder in the family (predispositional factor)
- Early loss (predispositional factor)
- Stress in life (provoking factor)

It is possible to describe the connection between the predispositional factors and the disease in terms of statistics. Such a factor may be the loss of a parent in childhood, the lack of peer support and intimate relationship, the disintegration of a family, unemployment, etc. [6].

Camberwel and Castello included the loss of a mother at an early age and three or more children. O'Neil et al. pointed out a positive family anamnesis, stress-laden lifestyle, the lack of peer support and intimate relationships as the major predispositional factors [6].

The research conducted by Brown, Harris, and Tennant revealed that the early loss of a mother is a major factor in leading to the emergence of depression in childhood or later. Tress demonstrated that adults suffering from neurotic disorders did not have a permanent person bringing them up when they were children [7].

Csorba and Huszár examined the family situation of girls threatened by suicidal tendencies. Twice as many girls with suicidal thoughts live in single-parent families than the members of the control group. Significant differences have been found in the family situation of the early childhood: many of the girls with suicide risks were brought up by one single parent or a relative [7].

The surveys conducted by Lloyd and Fukurawa demonstrated that negative experiences–e. g. separation from parents–before the age of 16 years were markedly more frequent in the research group than in the control group [6].

Palossari and Aro found a clear interrelation between susceptibility to depression and the divorce of parents when the children were very young [8].

Paykel et al. carried out research into the experiences of invididuals suffering from depression and found that patients had three times as many negative and adverse experiences in the six months preceding the appearance of their symptoms than the healthy people had. Often the adverse experience was the loss of a member of the family [9].

Abramson, as well as Brown and Harris, believes that life experiences function as provoking factors, and external events, triggering stress in the individual contribute to the manifestation of depression. The interpretation of these factors, however, depends on the preliminaries of the development of the personality concerned. A negative experience in life does not in itself generate depression, but it facilitates the appearance of the disease [4, 5, 6].

Richter's research revealed a positive connection between depression and the educational methods of the parents, especially the rejective and punitive attitudes of the parents [10].

Csorba and Huszár examined the educational methods of the parents of girls suffering from psychic distress, and found marked differences in the inconsistency, lack of acceptance, negligence and hostility of the parents [7].

Margitics has found a connection between certain family socializational factors–parental attitudes–and the emergence of depression syndrome. Out of the family socializational factors, the conflict-oriented family atmosphere, the lack of consistent educational attitude of the parents were the most important ones in connection with the appearance of depression syndrome. In the case of men, the factor responsible for the depression was the inconsistent educational attitude of the mother. Certain elements of the parental attitudes also show significant connections with depression. Interrelation with the lack of paternal love and care has been observable at both sexes, at women the lack of maternal love and overprotective attitude of the the mother has been also added [11].

Our research is to be focused on a more detailed examination of certain aspects of the predispositional factors as described in the related literature. These factors are regarded as responsible for the emergence of subclinical depression syndrome. We intend to conduct the research among college students.

An answer is sought as to whether it is possible to find any effect of predispositional factors in generating a susceptibility to depression in healthy, non-clinical college students whose socialization is largely successful and whose performance is accepted by society?

Our research has been based upon the following hypotheses:

1. The role of predispositional factors in the development of the personality of the individual is decisive, as the effect of these factors may appear later in life, so the subclinical depression syndrome (mild or medium depression on Beck's Depression Inventory) is observable at college students with any one of the predispositional factors:

- Positive family anamnesis (depression of father, mother, brother or sister or grandparents)
- Loss at an early age (loss of father or mother during the first 10 years of life)
- Longer (3-4 weeks) separation during the first 10 years of life
- Divorce of parents during the first 10 years of the life of the child
- More than one of the factors above.

2. The effect of predispositional loss (death of parent, separation, divorce) is more powerful if it happens very early in life.

3. Family socializational factors as well as parental treatment may function as predispositional factors.

2. METHOD

Participants

Data gathering took place at the College of Nyíregyháza, selecting students at random from all the faculties. Out of all the participants (n=681) 465 were women and 216 men. The average age was 19.98 years (standard deviation 1.51), with the median value of 20.

The research and control groups were set up according to the following criteria:

Those students were in the research groups, who had one of the following predispositional factors:

- Positive family anamnesis (medically diagnosed depression of mother, father, sibling or grandparent)
- Early loss in life (loss of father or mother in the first 10 years of age)
- Longer (3-4 weeks) separation during the first 10 years of life
- Divorce of parents during the first 10 years of the life of the child
- More than one of the factors above.
- No death occurred in the family or among close friends during the past half year (with this criterion we intended to exclude the effects of any normal mourning)

Students were arranged into the control group according to the following criteria:

- The effect of none of the predispositional factors was observable (no diagnosed depression patient in the family, spent their whole life in their original, complete families)
- No suicide occured in the direct family and among the close relatives during their life (this criterion is intended to minimize the chances of undiagnosed depression)
- Their stress load has been below average during the past half year, and scored median (-6) or lower in the Life Events Questionnaire.
- No death occurred in their families or among close relatives during the past half year (to exclude normal mourning reactions).

The sample thus set up was the following: 232 individuals (161 women, 71 men) were in the research group, and 219 individuals (135 women, 84 men) in the control group.

Measures

The following methods have been used for the personality analyses in both groups:

Survey of Risk Factors: Background Inquiry

A questionnaire for mapping the social background of the individual:

- Socio-demographic factors (gender, age, number of siblings)
- Socio-cultural factors (subject major learnt, place of residence)

- Family situation (present members of the family living in the same household, who were bringing them up in their first years, who were bringing them up in their childhood)
- Risk factors (if the father died, how old was he at that time, if the mother died, how old was she at that time; if the parents divorced, how old was the child at that time; has there been medically diagnosed depression in the family and if yes, who suffered from it; has suicide ever occurred in the family, and if yes, who committed it; has there been any separation longer than 3-4 years (e.g., period spent in hospital), and if yes, at what age?

The Secondary School Life Event Questionnaire, developed by Cohen et al. and its Hungarian adaptation by Csorba et al. [12, 13].

The data collected with these questionnaires made it possible to arrange the students into the two groups.

Survey of the Actual Symptoms of Depression

To study depression, we applied the Abridged screening version of Beck's Depression Inventory [14].

- The inventory studies the following components of depressive syndromes: sadness, pessimism, sense of failure, dissatisfaction, guilt, fear of punishment, suicide thoughts, indecisiveness, social withdrawal, self-image change, work difficulty, fatigability and anorexia.

Survey of Family Socialisation

We applied two different questionnaires:
The Hungarian adaptation of Goch's Family Socialisation Questionnaire [15].

- The questionnaire describes the following dimensions of family socialization: type of family atmosphere (rule-oriented or conflict oriented), the parenting aims (autonomy or conformity), the parenting attitudes (consistent, manipulative or inconsistent) and the style of parenting (supportive or reproving).

The Hungarian adaptation of the Parental Bonding Instrument [16] was the other instrument.

- The questionnaire has three main scales: love and care, overprotection and restriction, applied separately to the mother and the father.

The data collected have been processed with the help of SPSS for Windows 15.0 statistical software. In addition to the descriptive statistics, two paired t-test was used for a statistical comparative examination of the research and control groups.

3. RESULTS

The Depression Syndrome

Statistical data suggest that the control and research groups are markedly different in the aspects measured by Beck's Depression Inventory (F=35.35; t=9.61; p<0.000). The same is the situation when data are examined separately for women (F=26.41; t=8.603; p<0.000) and men F=7.115; t=4.169; p<0.000).

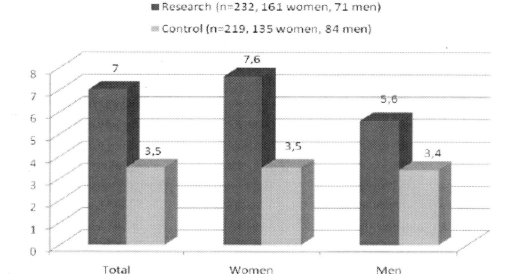

Figure 1. Results of the Research and Control Groups on Beck's Depression Inventory.

These results indicate that the predispositional factors do have their own effect in the case of non-clinical samples who are otherwise free of any clinical symptom, adaptive in their daily life and suffer from no significant disfunctions.

Out of the predispositional factors we paid special attention to the depression syndrome (figure 2).

The following factors were taken into consideration for the research:

- Positive family anamnesis, depression of father, mother, sibling, grandparents (N=102, 74 women, 28 men)
- Early loss; the loss of father or mother in the first 10 years of life (N=18, 11 women, 7 men)
- Longer (3-4 weeks) separation during the first 10 years (N=42, 29 women, 13 men)
- Divorce of parents during the first 10 years of the child (N=33, 21 women, 12 men)
- The individual was exposed to more than one of the negative effects above (N=35, 25 women, 10 men).

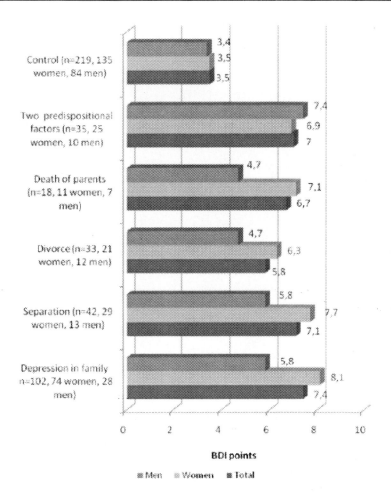

Figure 2. Results of the Research Group According to the Various Predispositional Factors on Beck's Depression Inventory.

When analysing the predispositional factors separately we find that the scores of the research group on Beck's Depression Inventory are significantly higher than those of the control group.

The persons with a positive family anamnesis (depression in the family) produced the highest number of points, which confirms the research findings of O'Neil et al. [6]. The second most powerful predispositional factor –in compliance with the results of Lloyd and Fukurawa [6]– a separation. The next in line is the early loss of parents, which is the same as what Brown, Harris, and Tennant found as a result of their own research [7]. Divorce appears to be the weakest predispositional factor, but even in this category the results still belong to the category of mild depression, as also indicated by Palossari and Aro [8].

When the two sexes are examined separately, the tendency is similar in the case of the women. Different is the situation in the men. They showed the highest number of points at two predispositional factors, while divorce and the death of parents did not occur as powerful predispositional factors.

An important result of our research is that it, demonstrating the powerful predispositional role of positive family anamnesis, confirms the findings of research projects that show the family cumulation of affective diseases [17].

The illness prevalence of the relatives and an earlier occurrence of the disease is observable in the generations born after 1945. This so-called cohort effect is not satisfactorily explained by changes in the gene frequency or the better diagnosis of the illness among young people [18].

At positive family anamneses, we examined whether the particular person suffering from depression has any connection with the depression syndrome (figure 3).

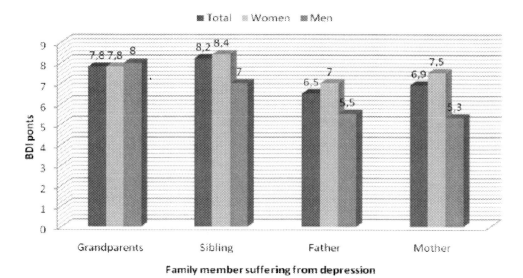

Figure 3. Results of the research group in a breakdown according to predispositional factors and age categories on Beck's Depression Inventory.

In 80 individuals (56 women, 24 men) the mother suffered from depression, in 12 individuals (8 women, 4 men) it was the father. The brother or sister of 27 (22 women, 5 men) individuals, and one of the grandparents of 15 persons (13 women, 2 men) suffered or suffers from depression.

A comparative statistical analysis (two paired t-test) has been carried out for each of the depressive groups (mother, father, sibling, grandparents), but no tangible difference has been found between the various groups. The statistical analysis of the two genders has produced a similar result. It means that in our case the coincidence of depression syndrome with a family anamnesis is independent of the particular member of the family suffering from depression.

The results above point towards genetical factors in the emergence of a susceptibility to depression, although in the case of affective diseases it is not possible to demonstrate a direct interrelationship between genotype and fenotype, as described in Mendel's rules of inheritance. It is not the disease itself that is inherited, but the dispositions that make the person susceptible to it. Susceptibility in itself is, however, not sufficient for the disease to develop. The disease is the result of complex genetical and environmental factors [17, 18].

We examined the relationship of predispositional factors and the age of the individuals.

Special attention has been paid to the death of the parents, separation and divorce of parents so as to find out if there is any connection between the gravity of the syndromes and the age of the children when they suffered the loss (figure 4).

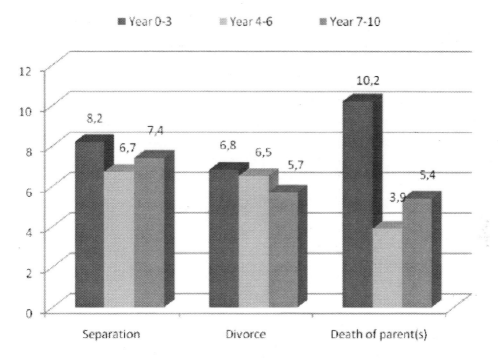

Figure 4. Results of the research group according to predispositional factors and age on Beck's Depression Inventory.

16 individuals suffered separation before they were three, the parents of 20 individuals divorced, and 6 of them lost one of their parents. The parents of 32 separated while their children were in kindergarten, and the parents of 19 divorced, and 7 lost one of their parents.

A comparative statistical analysis (two paired t-test) has been carried out for each of the depressive groups (0-3 years, 4-6 years, 7-10 years), but no tangible difference has been found between the various groups, except with the early death of a parent. The early death of parents (0-3 years) is a considerably more powerful predispositional factor than the same event in kindergarten age (F=1.69; t=3.138; p<0.009), or during the infant school (F=0.005; t=2.152; p<0.047). No difference has been revealed in the intensity of the predispositional factor when the death of the parent happened during the child's kindergarten or infant school years.

Family Socializational Effects

During the research we also examined the family socializational effects, as we believe that these may act as a predispositional factor and affect the depressive syndrome [11].

The present family circumstances of the individuals participating in the project have been analysed as well, in order to find out what correlations may be identified with their results on Beck's Depression Inventory.

At present 135 individuals (94 women, 41 men) live in their original, complete families, 24 of them (17 women, 7 men) live in complete families but with a foster father, 2 individuals (1 woman, 1 man) in a complete family but with foster mother, 54 indivuals (35 women, 19 men), live with their mother only, 6 of them (5 women, 1 men) live with their father, 3 individuals (2 women, 1 men), live with relatives, 8 of the group (7 women, 1 man) live on their own.

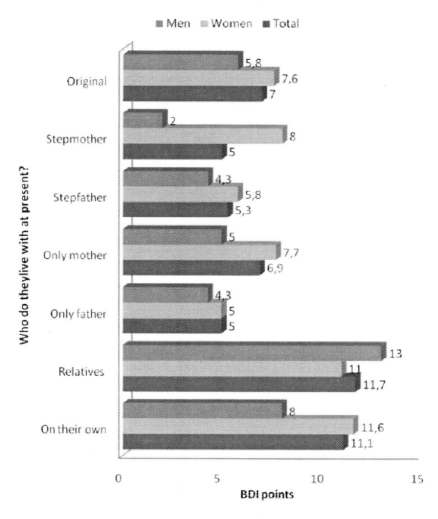

Figure 5. Results of the research group according to present family circumstances on Beck's Depression Inventory.

The proportion of those living in a family with a mother only is high, but if the figures are analysed in comparison with those living in complete families (figure 5) we find that two paired t-test shows no significant differences between their depression syndromes (F=1.066; T=0.246; p<0.806). The same is the case with the other family types, except those who live separately, who are markedly different from those living in their original families (F=2.682;

t=-2.411; p<0.017). The difference is, however, not explained by the higher stress generated by their independent status, as neither their objective stress load (number of negative experiences during the past half year), nor their subjective stress load (points for negative experiences) show any significant difference from those of the individuals living in their original families (no. of negative experiences: F=0.14; t=0.509; p<0.611; points for negative experiences: F=0.195; t=-0.305; p<0.224).

The presence of a permanent guardian in the first three years, and separately in the 4-10 years of the child marked the families of the students involved in the project.

In the first three years the majority of the individuals (209, 150 women, 59 men) were brought up by both parents. Only the mother was responsible for 17 children (8 women, 9 men), grandparents brought up 3 of the group (1 woman, 2 men), and foster parents were responsible for 1 individual (woman). 2 children lived in orphanages in this period (1 woman, 1 man).

When we analysed the possible inclination of the individuals living in their original and in single-parent families to depression syndrome, no considerable difference was found between the two groups (figure 6), neither for the whole of the sample (F=0.013; t=0.477; p<0.634), nor separately for women (F=0.24; t=395; p<0.693), and men (F=0.171; t=1.037; p<0.304). Because of the small number of individuals in the rest of the categories, the statistical comparative analyses have not been carried out.

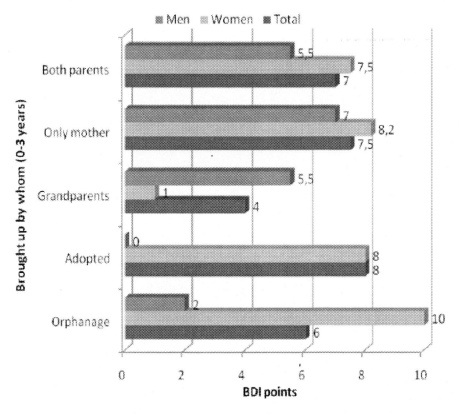

Figure 6. Results of the research group on Beck's Depression Inventory in a distribution according to who took care of the children during their first three years.

During the age from 4 to 10, 180 individuals (128 women, 52 men) were taken care of by both parents jointly. Only the mother was responsible for 45 of the group (28 women, 17 men), only the father for 2 (1 woman, 1 man), foster parents were bringing up 2 children (1 woman, 1 man), and relatives brought up 1 woman.

No considerable difference has been found between the two samples in this case either: $F=0.006$; $t=-0.625$; $p<0.532$. (women: $F=0.109$; $t=-0.136$; $p<0.892$, men: $F=0.000$; $t=-0.649$; $p<0.518$) (figure 7).

Because of the small number of individuals in the rest of the categories, the statistical comparative analyses have not been carried out.

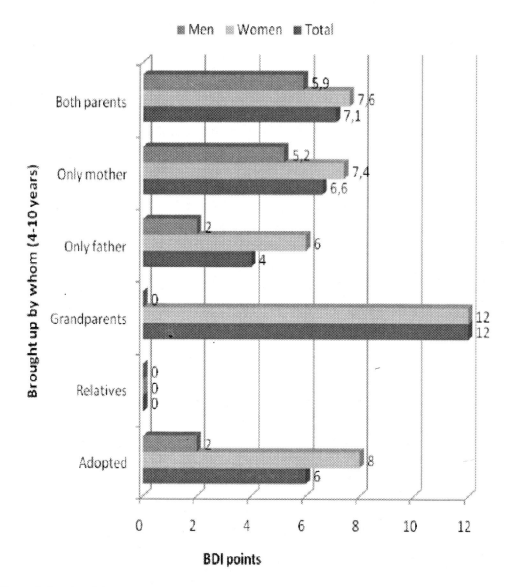

Figure 7. Results of the research group on Beck's Depression Inventory in a distribution according to who took care of the children when they were 4-10 years old.

An important element of family socialization is the educational effect of the parental treatment and educational methods.

In the course of our research we examined all the scales of the Family Socialization Questionnaire in order to survey their relationship with the depression syndrome (table 1).

In an examination of the family atmospheres in the two samples, a marked difference is observed in the conflict-oriented family atmosphere in the whole sample and separately for the men and women. It shows that a conflict-laden family atmosphere may develop into a predispositional factor in leading to the susceptibility to depression.

No noteworthy difference has been found in terms of educational objectives.

In the educational attitudes there are statistically observable differences between the two groups. There have been tangible differences at the manipulative and inconsistent educational attitudes, valid for the entire sample as a whole and separately to the two genders. It reinforces Adler's theory on depression. Adler claims that the depressive behaviour is a manipulative attempt at satisfying emotional claims (support, sympathy and assistance). A person suffering from depression considers approaches by other people as manipulative attempts, and becomes increasingly sensitive to such approaches. An individual suffering from depression will avoid responsibility and reciprocity for similar reasons. Such an individual is permanently preoccupied by the dilemma as to how long he/she is able to manipulate his/her environment without alienating other people. The constant manipulative struggles gradually become functionally autonomous, and develop into a lifestyle. Suffering is an inevitable and unpleasant consequence of this lifestyle. Adler considers the depressive symptoms as unconscious manipulative operations [19].

Considerable differences have been found at the maternal and paternal inconsistent educational attitudes and consistent educational attitudes. It coincides with the findings of Csorba, Huszár [7], and Margitics [11] in this field.

An Analysis of the Parental Treatment

When we analysed the parental treatment, we found significant interrelations between depression syndrome and predispositional factors at each point of the Parental Bonding Instrument (table 2).

From the aspect of the inclination to depression, the lack of maternal and paternal love and care, restriction, maternal and paternal overprotection all act as predispositional factors. A separate analysis of the two sexes shows the same factors in women, whereas in men significant interrelations have only been found with the lack of paternal love and care.

These results confirm the research findings of Parker and Perris, who argue that the disfunctional behaviour of the parent leads to the depression of the child when he/she grows up. They established that there is a close interrelation between insufficient parental care in childhood and depression in adulthood [6]. Women appear to be a lot more sensitive to this than men.

Table 1. Comparative statistics of the research and control groups in the Family Socializational Questionnaire (two paired t-test)

Scales of the Family Socializational Questionnaire	TOTAL			Women			Men		
	F	t	p<	F	t	p<	F	t	p<
Conflict-oriented family atmosphere	61,3	9,22	0,000	38,2	7,62	0,000	19,82	5,33	0,000
Manipulative educational attitude	41,31	6,21	0,000	28,54	5,3	0,000	13,92	3,49	0,001
Manipulative educational attitude (mother)	34,95	5,13	0,000	22,75	4,39	0,000	14,35	2,79	0,006
Manipulative educational attitude (father)	56,32	5,34	0,000	41,71	4,4	0,000	12,66	3,17	0,002
Supportive educational style	6,38	-4,66	0,000	17,66	-5,06	0,000	0,01	-1,46	n.s.
Supportive educational style (mother)	2,77	-2,81	0,905	12,06	-3,94	0,000	0,45	0,08	n.s.
Supportive educational style (father)	18,16	-4,96	0,000	22,64	-5,36	0,000	2,51	-1,29	n.s.
Punitive educational style	1,66	2,06	0,04	0,01	2,3	0,022	5,86	-0,07	n.s.
Punitive educational style (mother)	0,318	2,22	0,027	0,02	2,48	0,014	2,27	0,09	n.s.
Inconsistent educational attitude	54,36	6,1	0,000	49,13	6,04	0,000	8,68	2,04	0,04
Inconsistent educational attitude (mother)	36,84	4,95	0,000	37,36	4,72	0,000	4,46	1,74	n.s.
Inconsistent educational attitude (father)	48,39	5,03	0,000	49,71	5,21	0,000	6,01	1,26	n.s.
Consistent educational attitude	0,04	2,45	0,015	0,04	2,15	0,033	0,05	1,26	n.s.
Consistent educational attitude (mother)	0,025	1,88	n.s.	0,04	1,66	0,02	1,1		n.s.
Consistent educational attitude (father)	2,46	2,15	0,032	2,67	1,85	n.s.	1,08	1,32	n.s.

Table 2. Comparative statistics of the research and control groups in the Parental Bonding Instrument (two paired t-test)

SCALES OF THE QUESTIONNAIRE	TOTAL			Women			Men		
	F	t	p<	F	t	p<	F	t	p<
Mother: Love-care	25,94	-5,57	0,000	30,95	-5,38	0,000	0,25	-1,69	n. s.
Mother: Overprotection	8,47	3,75	0,000	6,63	4,03	0,000	2,01	0,64	n. s.
Mother: Restriction	0,18	-2,43	0,016	0,01	-3,4	0,001	0,07	0,96	n. s.
Father: Love-care	43,48	-6,67	0,000	30,59	-5,49	0,000	12,84	-4,03	0,000
Father: Overprotection	5,19	2,45	0,014	5,45	2,67	0,008	0,29	-0,54	n. s.
Father: Restriction	10,23	-3,15	0,002	7,01	-3,5	0,001	0,39	0,12	n. s.

4. DISCUSSION

Our research findings clearly justified our preliminary hypothesis, that is, predispositional factors relevant to inclination to depression are present at non-clinical populations (college students) as well. The effects of all predispositional factors (positive family anamnesis, death of parents, separation and divorce of the parents in the first ten years of the child) have been demonstrated. The family occurrence of depression proved to be the most powerful, pointing towards genetical factors in the emergence of susceptibility to depression. This concept is further supported by our finding that the predispositional power of the positive family anamnesis is independent of which particular member of the family suffered from depression. The complexity of the emergence of susceptibility to depression is indicated by the fact that the predispositional effect of environmental factors (death of parents, separation and the divorce of parents during the first ten years of the child) has also been clearly demonstrated.

We have not been able to convincingly justify the second hypothesis, supposing negative correlation between the power of the predispositional factor and the date of the loss (death of parents, separation and the divorce of parents during the first ten years of the child). In this respect, the only observable interrelation was detected between the death of the father and susceptibility to depression, and it was only present in men. It indicates the first ten years of a child is a uniformly sensitive period from the aspect of inclination to depression.

The third question, was whether there are family socializational factors, in addition to genetical causes, in the background of cumulation within a family? In our hypothesis we answered yes to this question, and we have been able to justify this. A conflict-laden family atmosphere, manipulative, inconsistent educational attitude, or the complete absence of an educational attitude are predispositional factors out of the elements of family socialization. At parental treatment, the lack of maternal and paternal love and care, the lack of restriction and both parental and maternal overprotection are all potential predispositional factors.

The research findings above confirm Szádóczky's opinion. Szádóczky asserts that depression should be regarded as a complex psycho-biological syndrome, the occurrence of which is the result of several factors, genetical, organic, psychological and social factors in various combinations [4].

The findings of our research – due to the limitations of the sample – cannot be generalised to and called valid for the present day Hungarian 18-23 year old youth. However, the results may also be useful in the wider area of prevention, promotion of adequate parental childcare views and the development of prevention forms which promote the healthy development of families.

REFERENCES

[1] Szádóczky, E. (2001): Epidemiológia. [Epidemology.] In E. Szádóczky, & Z. Rihmer (Eds.), *Hangulatzavarok* (pp.150-168). Budapest: Medicina Könyvkiadó.

[2] Kopp, M., & Szedmák, S., & Lőke, J., & Skrabski, Á. (1997). A depressziós tünetegyüttes gyakorisága és egészségügyi jelentősége a mai magyar lakosság körében. [The frequency and health importance of depression symptoms among the Hungarian population today.] *Lege Artis Medicine, 7*, 136-144.

[3] Rudolf, K.D., & Hammer, C. (1999). Age and gender as determinants of stress exposure, generation, and reactions in youngsters: A transactional perspective. *Child Development, 70*, 660-677.

[4] Szádóczky, E. (1998). Hangulatzavarok. [Disturbances in Mood.] In J. Füredi (Ed.), *A pszichiátria magyar kézikönyve* (pp.297-315). Budapest, Medicina Könyvkiadó.

[5] Herr, J., & Füredi, J. (2001). A család és a társadalom szerepe a depressziók kialakulásában és kezelésében. [The role of the family and the society in the emergence and treatment of depression.] *Nővér Praxis, 4,* 3-8.

[6] Herr, J. (2001). Pszichoszociális elméletek. [Psycho-social theories.] In E. Szádóczky, & Z. Rihmer (Eds.), *Hangulatzavarok* (pp.217-239). Budapest: Medicina Könyvkiadó.

[7] Csorba J., & Huszár, I. (1991). Szülőkapcsolat, nevelési jellemzők és társas támasz pszichés distresszben szenvedő serdülő lányoknál. [Parental Relationships, Educational Characteristics and Peer Group Support at Adolescent Girls Suffering from Psychic Distress.] *Pszichológia, 11,* 553-572.

[8] Palossari, U.K., & Aro, H.M. (1999). Parental divorce, self esteem and depression. An intimate relationship as a protective factor in young adulthood. *Journal of Affective Disorders, 35,* 91-96.

[9] Paykel, E.S., & Myers, J.K., & Dienel, T.M., & Klerman, G.L., & Lindenthal, J.J., & Pepper M.P. (1969). Live events and depression. *Archives of General. Psychiatry, 21,* 753-756.

[10] Csorba, J., & Papp, M., & Simon, L., & Simoni, S. (1998). Szülői attitüdök vizsgálata öngyilkossági kísérletet elkövetett serdülő lányoknál. [Parental Attitudes of Young Girls who have Attempted Suicide.] *Végeken, 9,* 4-9.

[11] Margitics, F. (2005). Prediszponáló tényezők kapcsolata a·szubklinikus depressziós tünetegyüttessel főiskolai hallgatóknál. [Interrelation between predisposition factors and sub clinical depression syndrome at college students.] *Psychiatria Hungarica, 20,* 211-223.

[12] Csorba, J., & Dinya, E., & Párt, S., & Solymos, J. (1994). Életesemény kutatás és serdülőkor. A középiskolás életesemény kérdőív bemutatása. [Life event research and adolescence. The Hungarian version of the Junior High Life Experiences Survey.] *Magyar Pszichológiai Szemle, 50,* 67-83.

[13] Csorba J., & Huszár, I. (1995). Életesemények vizsgálata serdülőkori szorongásos kórképekben. [Examination of life events in anxiety disorder syndromes in the case of adolescents.] *Gyermekgyógyászat. 46,* 133-139.

[14] Beck, A.T., & Beck R.W. (1972). Screening depressed patients in family practice. A rapid technique. *Postgraduate Medicine, 52,* 81-85.

[15] Sallay H., & Dabert C. (2001). The development of world beliefs in relation to parental education: the impact of being raised in a one-parent or an intact family. *X. Európai Fejlődéslélektani Konferencia*, Sweden, Uppsala, aug. 22-26.

[16] Tóth, I., & Gervai, J. (1999). Szülői Bánásmód Kérdőív (H-PBI): a Parental Bonding Instrument magyar változata. [Perceived parental styles: the Hungarian version of the Parental Bonding Instrument (H-PBI).] *Magyar Pszichológiai Szemle, 54,* 551-566.

[17] Trixler, M. (2001). A hangulatzavarok genetikája. [Genetics and Disturbances in Mood.] In E. Szádóczky, & Z. Rihmer (Eds,) *Hangulatzavarok* (pp.169-192). Budapest, Medicina Könyvkiadó.

[18] Alda, M. (1992). Az affektív betegségek genetikája. [Genetics and Affective Disorders] In: M. Arató (Ed.), *Depresszió* (pp. 11-22). Budapest: Cserépfalvi.

[19] Becker, J. (1989). *Depresszió. [Depression.]* Budapest: Gondolat.

Chapter 3

SURVEY OF THE BACKGROUND FACTORS OF SUBCLINICAL DEPRESSION SYNDROME IN THE CASE OF COLLEGE STUDENTS

ABSTRACT

In the course of our research we were seeking an answer to what backgrounds are in close interrelation with the subclinical depressive syndromes in college students, whose socialization can be considered successful, and who belong to the non-clinical population. We examined the following background factors: temperament and character features of personality, the dysfunctional attitudes, the coping strategies, the attributional style, as well as the factors of individual family socialization. 681 college students were involved in the research (465 women, and 216 men). The results of our research show that the lack of effective coping, some jeopardising factors of family socialisation, some attitudes becoming dysfunctional, and the passive attribution style have the closest interrelation with the depressive syndromes.

1. INTRODUCTION

Nowadays, depression may be considered a complex psychological syndrome, the development of which presumably several factors contribute, such as genetic, organic, psychological and social factors in a varied combination.

In accordance with the theory of vulnerability developed by Brown and Harris [1] depression emerges as a result of the interrelationship between the individual and his environment. The interaction and conjunction of predisposing factors and external conditions (provoking factors) are required for depression to develop.

The personal characteristics (self-esteem, self-power, conflict-solving strategies, anxiety bearing, ability to establish relationships, etc.), family background, evolution of personality, life style and social conditions altogether play a role in this predisposition. Life events function as provoking factors, and the external events may contribute to the manifestation of depression as stressors.

Several investigations have recently studied the correlation between the predisposing factors and the development of predisposition to depression. The findings of such surveys show that, among others, the early loss of mother [2], positive family anamnesis, early losses, stressful life and the lack of social support and intimate relations may have predisposing effects [3], as well as separation from parents [4, 5] or the divorce of parents, may have predisposing effect, if they occurred in childhood [6].

The researches carried out by Margitics, [7] unequivocally substantiated that predisposing factors (positive family anamnesis to depression, death of parents, separation and divorce in the first ten years of the child's life), which may be relevant in terms of the development of predisposition to depression – also have their impacts on the sample (college students) belonging to the non-clinical population.

In the "cognitive diathesis-stress model" of Garber and Hilsman [8], a style of negative attribution plays a key role in the formation of depressive symptoms in adolescents. It is presumed that the modelling of significant others, parental refusal and experiences with uncontrollable life events form the background for the development of the negative cognitive style.

In accordance with the findings Muris at al. [9] negative parental attributions are linked to depression through negative coping and low self-efficacy coping styles, and that negative parental rearing behaviour boosts this process in several ways among adolescents.

Several surveys have proved the links between negative coping style and depression. Results of Turner and his colleagues indicate that depression is negatively associated with problem-focused coping but positively with emotion-focused coping in the case of adults. Margitics [10] has also found the same in the course of researches made among college students. Herman-Stahl at al. [11], and Herman-Stahl and Petersen [12] revealed among adolescents that depressive symptomatology is accompanied by higher levels of passive and avoidant coping but lower levels accompany approach coping.

Several researches studied the interrelation between the parental rearing behaviour and depression. According to Parker at al. [13] investigations, neurotic depressive outpatients reported less parental care and greater maternal overprotection. In a further series of studies Parker [14] found the parental style of low care/high protection (affectionless-control) to be associated with an elevated risk for a number of neurotic disorders (depressive neurosis, anxiety neurosis, social phobia). Mackinnon at al. [15] in a research among non clinical population found that the lack of care rather than overprotection was the primary risk factor for depression. Narita at al. [16] found in a Japanese population that parental low care was always associated with having a lifetime history of depression. There was also evidence for the relationship between overprotective aspects of child-rearing behaviour and a lifetime history of depression. According to Birmaher at al. [17] it is essential to gain understanding of the links between diverse vulnerability factors.

The aim of this study is to reveal factors contributing to the development of depression under the aegis of complexity, in the case of non-clinical population. We intend to review the effects of the following: role of genetic and biological factors with the examination of temperament features; the role of the family socialization factors by surveying certain family socialisation effects and the parental rearing; the role of the socialisation factors with the examination of the dysfunctional attitudes, coping strategies, attributional styles and character features. Our goal is to reveal latent links of these background factors with the development of depression in college students.

2. METHOD

Participants

Data gathering took place at the College of Nyíregyháza, selecting students at random from all the faculties. Out of all the participants (n=681) 465 were women and 216 men. The average age was 19.98 years (standard deviation 1.51), with the median value of 20.

Measures

The following research methods were used:
Survey of the actual symptoms of depression:
To study depression, we applied the Abridged screening version of Beck's Depression Inventory [7, 18].

- The inventory studies the following components of depressive syndromes: sadness, pessimism, sense of failure, dissatisfaction, guilt, fear of punishment, suicide thoughts, indecisiveness, social withdrawal, self-image change, work difficulty, fatigability and anorexia.

According to the researches hitherto [19, 20] the abridged version comprising 13 items may be divided into two factors, somatic and and non-somatic factors. The factors of the somatic syndromes are composed of the work difficulty, the fatigability and anorexia. The surveys carried out by Margitics [7] have isolated two factors within the non-somatic factor: pure depression and the feeling of guilt. The following depressive syndromes belonged to the pure depression: sadness, pessimism, sense of failure, dissatisfaction, suicide thoughts and indecisiveness, while the feeling of guilt, fear of punishment and social withdrawal belonged to guilt.

Survey of the attitudes:
The Hungarian version of Weismann's Scale of Dysfunctional Attitudes [21, 22] was used.

- The scale included questions about the following attitudes: desire for external appraisal, need for affection, performance orientation, perfectionism, rightful and intensive requirements towards the environment, omnipotence (intensive altruism) and external control - autonomy.

Examination of coping strategies:
The Hungarian adaptation of Lazarus's Conflict Solving Questionnaire [22, 23].

- The following conflict solution strategies may be distinguished by means of the questionnaire: problem analysis, cognitive restructuring, adaptation (conformism), acting on emotional impetus, seeking emotional balance, withdrawal and asking for help.

Examination of the attributional style:

The Attributional Styles Questionnaire [24, 25] was used.

The following indices were used to judge attribution styles:

- External or internal attributions
- Unstable or stable attributions
- Specific or global attributions.

The persons participating in this study are asked to formulate a judgement of the following situations:

- Judgement of performance (failed to pass an exam)
- Judgement of loss (breaking up with a close friend).

Survey of family socialisation:

We applied two different questionnaires:

The Hungarian adaptation of Goch's Family Socialisation Questionnaire [26, 27, 28].

- The questionnaire describes the following dimensions of family socialization: type of family atmosphere (rule-oriented or conflict oriented), the parenting aims (autonomy or conformity), the parenting attitudes (consistent, manipulative or inconsistent) and the style of parenting (supportive or reproving).

The Hungarian adaptation of the Parental Bonding Instrument [29, 30] was the other instrument. This has three main scales: affection and care, overprotection and restriction.

Survey of temperament and character:

The Hungarian version of Cloninger's Temperament and Character Inventory adapted by Rózsa and his colleagues [31, 32] was filled in by the respondents. The main scales of the measure describes four temperament and three character dimensions:

- The temperament-scales are: novelty seeking, harm avoidance, reward dependence, persistence
- The character-scales are: self-directedness, cooperativeness, self-transcendence.

3. RESULTS

The data were processed by means of the SPSS for Windows 15.0 statistical program. In addition to the descriptive statistics and the linear regression analysis of several aspects, the survey of the background was made by us by means of factor analysis (main component factor analysis, varimax rotation procedure).

Primarily those elements of the surveyed factors (dysfunctional attitudes, coping strategies, attributional styles, family socialisation factors, personality's temperament and character features) were involved in the scope of research that were in significant correlation with depressive syndromes in accordance with the results of the linear regression analysis. These are illustrated in table 1 below.

Table 1. Factors closely and significantly associated with depressive syndromes

Inquiries	Scales of Inquiries	$p<$
Dysfunctional Attitudes Scale	External control attitude	0.000
	Need for affection	0.032
	Need for external appraisal	0.027
	Perfectionism	0.019
Conflict Solving Questionnaire	Cognitive restructuring	0.000
	Conformism	0.012
	Acting on emotional impetus	0.000
	Withdrawal	0.000
	Asking for help	0.004
Attributional Styles Questionnaire	Endeavour to stability in the case of performance deficit	0.009
	Endeavour to globality in the case of performance deficit	0.000
	Endeavour to globality in the case of loss	0.049
Family Socialization Questionnaire	Conflict oriented family atmosphere	0.000
Parental Bonding Instrument	Maternal affection and care	0.002
	Maternal overprotection	0.025
	Paternal affection and care	0.000
Temperament and Character Inventory	Harm avoidance	0.000
	Self-directedness	0.000
	Self-transcendence	0.010

We unveiled the latent correlations between the examined factors related to depressive syndromes by means of factor analysis. When differentiating among the background factors we considered for the survey, in accordance with the common practice, only the rotated factors having a factor loading not lower than 0.4. (see table 2).

Table 2. On the basis of linear regression analysis the structuring of factors showing significant relations with depressive syndromes relying on the secondary factor analysis (l>0.40)

	Factors					
	1	2	3	4	5	6
Father: affection-care	-.801					
Conflict oriented family atmosphere	.786					
Mother: affection-care	-.644					
Acting on emotional impetus						
Need for external appraisal		.712				
Perfectionism		.636				
Need for affections		.618				
External control attitude		.595	'			
Asking for help			.817			
Withdrawal			.736			
Conformism			.447			
Harm avoidance				-.707		
Cognitive restructuring				.696		
Self-directedness				.645		

Table 2. (Continued).

	Factors					
	1	2	3	4	5	6
Loss: global attribution					.763	
Performance: global attribution					.689	
Performance: stabile attribution					.539	
Mother: overprotection						.753
Self-transcendence						.524

The results of the principal component analysis showed that the examined variables were grouped under six factors which explained 52.2 percent of the total variance.

The first factor (eigenvalue: 3.55) explained 18.7 percent of the complete variance, and marks the lack of maternal and paternal affection and care, and is accompanied by conflict-ridden family atmosphere. This may also be referred to as *the factor of hazardous family socialisation factor.*

The second factor (eigenvalue: 1.848) explained 9.7 percent of the total variance and describes dysfunctional attitudes. This may be called *the factor of dysfunctional attitudes.*

The third factor (eigenvalue: 1.642) explained the 8.7 percent of the total variance, and demonstrates the scoping strategies (asking for help, withdrawal, conformism), and is referred to as *the factor of searching for support.*

The fourth factor (eigenvalue: 1.24) explained 6.5 percent of the total variance, and shows the features of personality (lack of harm avoidance and the ability for self-directedness), being accompanied by the ability for cognitive restructuring. This may be referred to as *the factor of effective coping.*

The fifth factor (eigenvalue: 1.149) explained 6.1 percent of the total variance, and marks the *passive attributional style.*

The sixth factor (eigenvalue:1.054) explained 5.5 percent of the total variance, and demonstrates the maternal overprotection, which is accompanied by the higher level of self-transcendence. This is referred to as *the factor of maternal overprotection.*

Table 3 demonstrates how closely the individual factors of Beck's Depression Inventory were related on the basis of the results obtained with the linear regression analysis with the individual latent background factors disclosed.

Table 3. Beck's Depression Inventory (Pearson correlation between the individual factors with the latent background factors)

Factors	Factors of Beck's Depression Inventory		
	Pure depression	Feeling of guilt	Somatic
Imperilling family socialisational factors	0,232**	0,122**	0.050
Dysfunctional attitudes	0,104**	0,177**	0.087*
Search for support	0,039	0,135**	0.042
Effective coping	-0,034**	-0,175**	-0.205**
Passive attributional style	0,121**	0,172**	0.171**
Maternal overprotecting	0129**	0,108**	0.057

** Correlation is significant at the 0.01 level

* Correlation is significant at the 0.05 level.

From among the individual factors of Beck's Depression Inventory the feeling of guilt showed the closest correlation with the background factors, being strongly and significantly associated with each of them.

Except from the factor of searching for support the pure depression also showed a close relation to each background factor. The loosest correlation emerged in the case of the somatic factor, which had significant relation only to dysfunctional attitudes, pessimistic attribution style, and a deficit of effective coping.

We also examined by means of the linear regression analysis the strength of correlation of the individual items in Beck's Depression Inventory. This showed the defined background factors depicted in. table 4.

Table 4. Characteristics of Pearson correlation between depressive syndromes and the latent background factors

Items of Beck's Depression Inventory	Imperilling family socialisation factors	Dysfunctional attitudes	Search for support	Effective coping	Passive attributional style	Maternal overprotecting
Sadness	0.136**	0.153**	0.131**	-0.272**	0.171**	0.106**
Pessimism	0.108**	0.137**	0.084*	-0.339**	0.099**	0.105**
Sense of failure	0.241**	0.101**	-0.008	-0.298**	0181**	0.135**
Dissatisfaction	0.106**	0.101**	-0.012	-0.227**	0.087*	0.110**
Feeling of Guilt	0.154**	0.163**	0.099**	-0246**	0.201**	0.116**
Fear of punishment	0.114**	0.101**	0.080*	-0.144**	0.148**	0.091*
Self-harm	0.241**	0.109**	0.084*	-0150**	0.131**	0.139**
Social withdrawal	0.123**	-0.012	-0.001	-0246**	0.054	0.046
Indecisiveness	0.040	0.127**	0.121**	-0250**	0.110**	0.108**
Self-image change	0.161**	0.198**	0.112**	-0206**	0.133**	0.036
Work difficulty	0.169**	0.084*	0.060	-257**	0.199**	0.067
Fatigability	0.66	0.039	0.066	-0211**	0.159**	0.121**
Anorexia	0.95*	0.151**	-0.009	-0.095*	0.131**	0.013

** Correlation is significant at the 0.01 level

* Correlation is significant at the 0.05 level.

The lack of effective coping showed the closest correlation to depressive syndromes, which was significantly associated with each inspected syndrome without any exception.

Passive attributional style also showed a close relation with the depressive syndromes and it was in close correlation with all the syndromes except for apathy.

Hazardous family socialisation factors were not associated with indecisiveness and fatigability, while the dysfunctional attitudes were not correlated with the social withdrawal and fatigability.

Of the studied from background factors only maternal overprotection and the search for support showed no close relation to the depressive syndromes. Maternal overprotecting showed no close correlation with social withdrawal, self-image change, work difficulties and anorexia, while the search for support was not closely associated to sense of failure, dissatisfaction, social withdrawal, work difficulties, fatigability and anorexia.

4. DISCUSSION

With our research, beyond the effects of the predisposing factors, we managed to indicate the roles of several other background factors in the development of depressive syndromes.

The lack of coping efficacy showed the closest correlation with the formation of depressive syndromes. The central element in this is the person's insufficient ability to cognitively restructure the situation, which was associated with the personality temperament factors of high level of harm avoidance and the low level of self-directedness. The lack of cognitive restructuring means that the person is not capable of reconstructing the situation in hardships, and thus cannot move to a higher level of personality development [33].

Persons who are characterised by a high level of harm avoidance are pessimistic, careful, shy, anxious, fear of dangers and risks, are reserved, inhibited and fatigue easily. Low self-directedness may refer to immature personality. The self-esteem of such persons is low, feels his life meaningless, is undisciplined, aimless, accuser, and blames his environment for his failures [32].

The lack of maternal and paternal affection and care as key elements of hazardous family socialisation were directly related to the development of depressive syndromes and were associated with conflict-ridden family atmosphere.

Furthermore, the results of our researches showed that some attitudes becoming dysfunctional may also contribute to the development of depressive syndromes. Of these dysfunctional attitudes the following are the most salient, and are in accordance with the data of literary sources: intensive external control attitude, need for affection, need for external appraisal, and perfectionism.These may directly lead to the development of depressive syndromes.

Eventually, according to our findings, pessimistic attribution style may also make a person predisposed to the appearance of depressive syndromes. The stability (it will be always like this) and globality (anything I do, I make it wrong) of the reason concerned had a predominant role in this.

The background factors referred to by us as search for support and maternal overprotecting also had a direct correlation with the depressive syndromes.

Diverse coping strategies came to the surface in the case of the search for support. Asking for help had a considerable weight as a factor, showing that the person tries to cope with difficult situations by applying these strategies. Another strong within background variable was withdrawal, but conformity was somewhat less significant still having a considerable factor weight. Apparently the failure to receive help may lead either to withdrawal or unsteady conformity.

Maternal overprotecting may also lead to the appearance of depressive syndromes, as it makes the personality sensitive to external influences and vulnerable, as well as being inclined to protective withdrawal. Thus in this background factor we may see and interpret the role of the self-transcendence as character dimension related to maternal overprotecting.

The results of our researches proved the complexity of the development of depression. Findings of our surveys may be applied efficiently primarily in the field of prevention, and in the course of the imperilled persons' therapies.

References

[1] Brown, G W., & Harris, T. (1986). Establishing Causal Links, The Bedford College Studies of Depression. In H. Kasching (Ed.), *Life Events and Psychiatric Disorders.* London-Cambridge: University Press.

[2] Costello, C.G. (1982). Social Factors Associated With Depression: Retrospective Community Study. *Psychological Medicine, 12,* 329-339.

[3] O'Neil, M.K., & Lancee, W.J., & Stanly, J., & Freeman, J. (1986). Psychosocial Factors and Depressive Symtoms. *Journal of Nervous and Mental Diseases, 11,* 15—22.

[4] Lloyd, C. (1980). Life Events As Predisposing Factors. *Archives of General Psychiatry, 37,* 529—535.

[5] Furukawa, T.A., & Ogura, A., & Hirai, T., & Fujihara, S., & Kitamura, T., & Takahasi, K. (1999). Early Parental Separation Experiences Among Patients With Bipolar Disorder and Major Depression: Case Control Study. *Journal of Affective Disorders, 54,* 85-91.

[6] Palosaari, U.K., & Aro, H.M. (1999). Parental divorce, self esteem and depression. An intimate relationship as a protective factor in young adulthood. *Journal of Affective Disorders, 35,* 91-96.

[7] Margitics, F. (2005). Prediszponáló tényezők kapcsolata a szubklinikus depressziós tünetegyüttessel főiskolai hallgatóknál. [Interrelation between predisposition factors and subclinical depression syndrome at college students.] *Psychiatria Hungarica, 20,* 211-223.

[8] Garber, J., & Hilsman, R. (1992). Cognition, stress, and depression in children and adolescents. *Child and Adolescent Psychiatric Clinics of North America, 1,* 129-167.

[9] Muris, P., & Schmid, T.H., & Lambrichs, R., & Meesters, C. (2001). Protective and vulnerability factors of depression in normal adolescents. *Behaviour Research and Therapy, 3,* 555-565.

[10] Margitics F. (2005). A diszfunkcionális attitűdök, megküzdési stratégiák és az attribúciós stílus összefüggése a szubklinikus depressziós tünetegyüttessel főiskolai

hallgatóknál. [Interrelations between dysfunctional attitudes, coping strategies and attributional style and subclinical depressive syndrome at college students.] *Mentálhigiéné és Pszichoszomatika, 6,* 95-122.

[11] Herman-Stahl, M.A., & Stemmler, M., & Petersen, A.C. (1995). Approach and avoidant coping: Implications for adolescents mental health. *Journal of Youth and Adolescence, 24,* 649-665.

[12] Herman-Stahl, M.A., & Petersen, A.C. (1996). The protective role of coping and social resources for depressive symptoms among young adolescents. *Journal of Youth and Adolescence, 25,* 733-753.

[13] Parker, G. (1979). Parenthal characteristics in relation to depressive disorders. *British Journal of Psychiatry, 134,* 138-147.

[14] Parker, G. (1983). Parental „affectionless control" as an antecedent to adult depression. A risk factor delineated. *Archives of General Psychiatry, 40,* 956-960.

[15] Mackinnon, A.J., & Henderson, A.S., & Andrews, G. (1993). Parental „affectionless control" as an antecedent to adult depression: a risk factor refined. *Psychological Medicine, 23,* 135-141.

[16] Narita, T., & Sato, T., & Hirano, S., & Gota, M., & Sakado, K., & Uehara, T. (2000). Parental child-rearing behavior as measured the Parental Bonding Instrument in a Japanese population: factor structure and relationship to a lifetime history of depression. *Journal of Affective Disorders, 57,* 229-234.

[17] Birmaher, B., & Ryan, N.D., & Williamson, D E., & Brent, D.A., & Kaufman, J., & Dahl, R.E., & Perel, J., & Nelson, B. (1996). Childhood and adolescent depression: A review of the past 10 years. Part I. *Journal of the American Academy of Child and Adolescent Psychiatry, 35,* 1427-1439.

[18] Beck, A.T., & Beck R.W. (1972). Screening depressed patients in family practice. A rapid technique. *Postgraduate Medicine, 52,* 81-85.

[19] Vrendenburg, K., & Kramels, L., & Flett, G L. (1985). Re-examining the Beck Depression Inventory: the long and short of it. *Psychological Reports, 56,* 767-778.

[20] Volk, R.J., & Pace, T.M., & Parchmann, M.L. (1993). Screening for depression in primary care patients: dimensionality of short of the Beck Depression Inventory. *Psychological Assessment, 5,* 173-181

[21] Weisman, A.N., & Beck, A.T. (1979). *The Dysfunctional Attitude Scale.* Thesis, University of Pennsylvania.

[22] Kopp, M. (1994). *Orvosi pszichológia. [Medical psychology.]* Budapest: SOTE Magatartástudományi Intézet.

[23] Folkmann, S., & Lazarus, R.S. (1980). An analysis of coping in a middle-aged community sample. *Journal of Health and Social Behaviour, 21,* 219-239.

[24] Peterson, C., & Semmel, A., & von Baeyer, C., & Abramson, L.Y., & Metalsky, G.I., & Seligman, M.E.P. (1982). The Attributional Style Questionnaire. *Cognitive Therapy and Research, 6,* 287-299.

[25] Atkinson, R.L, & Atkinson, R.C., & Smith, E.E., & Bem, D.J. (1995): *Pszichológia. [Psychology.]* Budapest: Osiris.

[26] Goch, I. (1998): *Entwicklung der Ungewissheitstoleranz. Die Bedeutung der familialen Socialization.* Regensburg: Roderer.

[27] Sallay, H., & Dabert, C. (2002). Women's perception of parenting: a German-Hungarian comparison. *Applied Psychology in Hungary, 3-4,* 55-56.

[28] Sallay, H., & Krotos, H. (2004). Az igazságos világba vetett hit fejlődése: japán és magyar kultúrközi összehasonlítás. [Evolution of belief in a fair world: Japanese and Hungarian intercultural comparison.] *Pszichológia, 24,* 233-252.

[29] Parker, G., & Tupling, H., & Brown, L. B. (1979). A Parental Bonding Instrument. *British Journal of Medicinal Psychiatry, 52,* 1-10.

[30] Tóth, I., & Gervai, J. (1999). Szülői Bánásmód Kérdőív (H-PBI): a Parental Bonding Instrument magyar változata. [Perceived parental styles: the Hungarian version of the Parental Bonding Instrument (H-PBI).] *Magyar Pszichológiai Szemle, 54,* 551-566.

[31] Cloninger, C.R. (1987). A systematic method for clinical description and classification of personality variants. *Archives of General Psychiatry, 44,* 573-588.

[32] Rózsa S., & Kállai, J., & Osváth, A., & Bánki M. Cs. (2005). *Temperamentum és karakter: Cloninger pszichobiológiai modellje. A Cloninger-féle temperamentum és karakter kérdőív felhasználói kézikönyve. [Temperament and character. Cloninger's psychobiologycal model. The handbook of the Cloninger Temperament and Character Inventory.]* Budapest: Medicina Könyvkiadó Rt.

[33] Kopp, M. (2001). Magatartástudományi ember-környezeti rendszerelméleti modell. [Behavioral scientific human-environmental system theoretical model.] In B. Buda, & M. Kopp & E. Nagy (Eds.), *Magatartástudományok [Behavioral Scient]* (pp. 23-46.). Budapest: Medicina.

Chapter 4

THE ROLE OF RISK AND PROTECTIVE SOCIALISATION FACTORS IN THE CASE OF PERSONS WITH VULNERABILITY TO DEPRESSION

ABSTRACT

The aim of this research was to discover in a group of young, healthy people (college students) not belonging to the clinical population, the risk and protective factors having a role in the development of predisposition to depression and being related to family socialisation factors. The sample was taken on the basis of the existence or lack of predisposing factors (positive family anamnesis to depression, death of parents, separation and divorce in the first ten years of the child's life): 232 persons belonged to the group of imperilled people (161 women, 71 men), and 219 persons were in the control group (135 women, 84 men). The group of imperilled persons were further divided on the basis of the results achieved in Beck's Depression Inquiry (BDI) for a group of normal level (n=104, 63 women, 41 men) and a high level depression (n=128, 98 women, 30 men) group. For the examination of the family socialisation effects, we used Goch's Family Socialisation Inquiry, and the Hungarian adaptation of the Parental Bonding Instrument developed by Parker et al. On grounds of a non-clinical sample our survey substantiated that certain family socialisation factors may also play a role as risk and protective factors in the development of depression particularly in the case of vulnerable persons. We managed to substantiate that the primary risk factors were the punishing and neglecting way of breeding by parents, the manipulative, inconsistent and consistent educational attitudes, the conflict filled family attitude, and several elements of parental treatment (restriction, lack of affection and care, intensified overprotection). We managed to indicate as protective factor the defending effect, principally, of the supportive and less punishing educational style of parents, the lack of manipulative and inconsistent educational attitude, the tranquil family atmosphere, the homogeneous parental breeding, as well as the paternal treatment showing affection, care, restrictions but less over-protection.

1. INTRODUCTION

The predisposing and provoking psycho-social factors also contribute in a significant extent to the development of depression. According to the vulnerability theory of Brown and Harris [1] three basic psycho-social factors play an essential role in the development of predisposition to depression: the appearance of the disorder in the family (predisposing factor), early-age loss (predisposing factor) and stressful life (provoking factor).

Several examinations have studied recently the correlation between the predisposing factors and the development of predisposition to depression. The findings of such surveys show that, among others, the early loss of mother [2] the positive family anamnesis, early losses, the stressful life and the lack of social support and intimate relations may have predisposing effects [3] as well as the separation from the parents [4, 5] or the divorce of parents, if such things occurred in childhood [6].

The researches carried out by Margitics [7] substantiated unequivocally – corresponding to the data found in literature – that the predisposing factors (positive family anamnesis to depression, death of parents, separation and divorce in the first ten years of the child's life), which may be relevant in terms of the development of predisposition to depression – also have their impacts on the sample (college students) belonging to the non-clinical population.

In families from lower social levels, according to researches, the children are exposed to higher stress and this may contribute to the development of the symptoms of depression [8, 9]. As an effect of hard financial conditions of the family and due to pecuniary problems the symptoms of depression in the case of adolescents also appear more often [10].

The dysfunctional actions of the parent may also predispose to adult age depression already in the childhood in the case of persons who are inclined to that [11]. Conflicts in family, bad relationship with or between the parents, the lack of trust or maltreatment by the parent may lead to the symptoms of depression in adolescent age [12].

Other researches found positive interrelation between depression and the breeding techniques of parents, particularly between rejecting and punishing parental methods, as well as in the field of inconsistency, the lack of acceptance, neglect and malignancy on the parents' side [13, 14].

The foregoing highlight the fact that we must know the psychosocial factors – both for the purpose of efficient healing and for prevention - that may contribute to the development of depression, or that may act as protecting factors in the preservation of mental health [15].

Surveys made among healthy young people not with diagnostic but with primary preventive purposes may provide assistance for the experts of mental hygiene in their work for health improvement by discovering the risk groups and menacing factors. Through the early recognition of the non-clinical forms of depression the prevention of more serious forms of the disease may be implemented [15].

The aim of the risk and protective theory is to define the major risk and protective factors, that on the one hand endanger mental health, on the other hand serve as protective factors for the prevention [15, 16, 17].

Our aim with this survey was to discover among healthy young people belonging to the non-clinical population (college students) the risk and protective factors playing a role in the development of predisposition to depression and being related to the family socialisation factors. We intend to contribute with the results of the examination to the effectiveness of preventive programs dealing with the mental health of the youth, and to provide new information for the experts working with families.

2. METHOD

Participants

Data gathering took place at the College of Nyíregyháza, selecting students at random from all the faculties. Out of all the participants (n=681) 465 were women and 216 men. The average age was 19.98 years (distribution 1.51), with the median value of 20.

When inspecting the risk factors those students were put in the group of imperilled persons in the case of whom any of the following predisposing factors were present: positive family anamnesis (clinically diagnosed depression in the case of the father, mother, sibling, grandparent); suffered losses in their early age (death of mother or father, divorced parents in the first ten years of life of the child); suffered longer (3-4 weeks) separation during the first ten years of their lives; suffered more than one of the mentioned negative effects; during the past half a year no decease happened in their families, or among close relatives and friends (we intended to exclude by this criterion the effect of normal mourning reaction). Those students were put in the control group in the case of whom no effect of any predisposing factor could be detected (no clinically diagnosed depression occured in their families, they have lived their whole life in the complete and original family; no suicide happened among the close relatives (father, mother, sibling, grandparent), we intended to minimise through this criterion the effects of un diagnosed depression; the stress load was below the average during the past half a year, the median in the Lifetime Events Inquiry reached (-6), or a lower point (exclusion of the provocative factors); no deaths occurred in their families during the past half a year, neither among the close relatives or friends (exclusion of the normal mourning reaction).

The sample developed in accordance with the aforementioned criteria had the following composition: 232 persons belonged to the group of imperilled persons (161 females, 71 males), and 219 persons were in the control group (135 females, 84 males).

During the survey of the protective factors the group of imperilled people was further divided on the basis of the results they achieved with Beck's Depression Inquiry (BDI), with the consideration of the following criteria:

Those students were put in the group showing normal depression level whose results were between 0 and 5 points (n=104, 63 females, 41 males).

Those students were put in the group showing an increased level of depression whose results were over 5 points (n=128, 98 females, 30 males).

Measures

The following research methods were used:
Survey of risk factors: Background Inquiry.

The inquiry was to give a clear view of the following fields of the social background of the person filling in the Inquiry: socio-demographic factors (sex, age, number of siblings); socio-cultural factors (faculty attended, domicile); family situation (with whom from the family do they live at present, who brought them up in the first years of their lives, who brought them up in their childhood); risk factors: (if the father died, how old was the person at the time of the father's death; if the mother died, how old was the person at the time of the mother's death; if the parents got divorced, how old was the person at the time of divorce, has depression been diagnosed clinically in the family, if yes, with whom; has suicide ever happened in the family, if yes who committed it; has the person ever spent longer period (3-4 weeks) separated by force from the family (e.g. in hospital), if yes, at what age).

Survey of the actual symptoms of depression:

To study depression, we applied the Abridged screening version of Beck's Depression Inventory [18].

- The inventory studies the following components of depressive syndromes: sadness, pessimism, sense of failure, dissatisfaction, guilt, fear of punishment, suicide thoughts, indecisiveness, social withdrawal, self-image change, work difficulty, fatigability and anorexia.

Survey of family socialisation:

We applied two different questionnaires:

The Hungarian adaptation of Goch's Family Socialisation Questionnaire [19, 20, 21].

- The questionnaire describes the following dimensions of family socialisation: type of the family atmosphere (rule oriented family atmosphere, conflict oriented family atmosphere), breeding target (breeding for autonomy, autonomy as a target of breeding, breeding for conformity, conformity as a breeding target), educational attitudes (consistent educational attitude, manipulative educational attitude, inconsistent educational attitude) and the educational style (supporting educational style, punishing educational style).

The Hungarian adaptation of the Parental Bonding Instrument [22, 23] was the other instrument.

- The questionnaire has three main scales: love and care, overprotection and restriction, applied separately to the mother and the father.

Survey of lifetime events:

Secondary School Lifetime Event Inquiry developed by Cohen et al., the Hungarian version adapted by Csorba et al. [11].

Besides descriptive statistics, we applied two paired t-test for the comparative statistical analysis of the test group and the control group. Data were processed by means of the SPSS for Windows 15.0 statistical program package.

Table 1. Descriptive and comparative statistics of the results achieved in the Family Socialisation and Parental Bonding Instrument by the control group and the test group

Scales of Family Socialisation Questionnaire	AGGREGATE			FEMALES			MALES		
	Imperilled Group	Control Group	P<	Imperilled Group	Control Group	P<	Imperilled Group	Control Group	P<
Conflict oriented family atmosphere	M=13.6 SD=5.7	M=9.5 SD=3.5	0,000	M=13.8 SD=5.8	M=9.4 SD=3.7	0,000	M=13.3 SD=5.4	M=9.6 SD=3.1	0,000
Manipulative educational attitude	M=12.2 SD=6.3	M=9.1 SD=3.8	0,000	M=11.9 SD=6.4	M=8.7 SD=3.5	0,000	M=12.8 SD=6.1	M=9.8 SD=4.2 -	0,001
Supportive educational style	M=27.4 SD=6.9	M=30.2 SD=5.9	0,000	M=27.5 SD=6.7	M=31.1 SD=5.2	0,000	M=27 SD=7.3	M=28.7 SD=6.6	n. s.
Punishing educational style	M=17.4 SD=5.3	M=16.4 SD=5.6	0,040	M=17.7 SD=5.5	M=16.2 SD=5.5	0,022	M=16.7 SD=4.8	M=16.7 SD=5.8	n. s.
Inconsistent educational attitude	M=8.2 SD=4.6	M=6 SD=2.9	0,000	M=8.5 SD=4.7	M=5.8 SD=2.7	0,000	M=7.5 SD=4.4	M=6.3 SD=3.1	0,040
Consistent educational attitude	M=12.1 SD=5	M=10.9 SD=5	0,015	M=11.8 SD=4.9	M=10.6 SD=4.8	0,033	M=12.6 SD=5.2	M=11.6 SD=5.3	n. s.
Maternal affection-care	M=29.6 SD=6.8	M=32.6 SD=4.3	0,000	M=29 SD=7.5	M=32.9 SD=4.5	0,000	M=30.8 SD=4.8	M=32 SD=4.1	n. s.
Maternal overprotection	M=6 SD=4.7	M=4.5 SD=3.7	0,000	M=6.4 SD=4.8	M=4.3 SD=3.9	0,000	M=5.2 SD=4.5	M=4.8 SD=3.7	n. s.
Maternal restriction	M=10.2 SD=3.7	M=11.1 SD=3.6	0,016	M=9.6 SD=3.5	M=11 SD=3.6	0,001	M=11.6 SD=3.7	M=11.1 SD=3.5	n. s.
Paternal affection-care	M=24.2 SD=9.5	M=29.4 SD=6.4	0,000	M=24.1 SD=9.8	M=29.6 SD=6.6	0,000	M=24 SD=8.9	M=29.1 SD=6.1	0,000
Paternal overprotection	M=4.8 SD=4.6	M=3.7 SD=3.9	0,014	M=5.3 SD=4.9	M=3.9 SD=4.1	0,008	M=3.2 SD=3.4	M=3.5 SD=3.5	n. s.
Paternal restriction	M=10.5 SD=4.6	M=11.8 SD=3.796	0,002	M=10 SD=4.6	M=11.7 SD=3.8	0,001	M=11.8 SD=4.2	M=11.8 SD=3.8	n. s.

M=mean value, SD=standard deviation, P= probability for exceeding, n.s.= not significant.

3. RESULTS

During the survey of the risk factors we analysed all scales of the Family Socialisation and Parental Bonding Instrument to discover the interrelationship between them and the depressive syndromes.

In accordance with the data indicated in table 1, it is apparent that strong and significant deviations were found in many fields between the imperilled group and the control group based on each scale of the two inquiries (only those scales are represented in the Table for which significant differences were discovered between the two mentioned groups).

Examining the family atmosphere in the two mentioned groups, we found significant deviations regarding the conflict-oriented family atmosphere. The members of the imperilled group, independent of their sex, perceived that the atmosphere of their family was strained with more conflicts than the families of the control group members.

No remarkable differences were found by us in terms of breeding targets between the two groups.

An obvious deviation considering the educational attitudes was revealed between the two groups with respect to the manipulative educational attitude that was typical of the imperilled group both regarding the whole sample and for the sexes respectively. It is interesting that the members of both groups perceived their mothers to be more manipulative than their fathers. Another significant difference was between the maternal and paternal inconsistent educational attitude, as well as in the field of consistent educational attitude, which was also a characteristic typical to the parents of the persons belonging to the group of imperilled students. Regarding the sexes, such differences were revealed only in the case of women, and we found that such educational attitudes were even more typical to the parents of the students in the group of imperilled persons. Regarding the mentioned attitudes considerable differences concerning the maternal and paternal educational attitudes were not found in either of the groups.

In terms of the educational style the members of the group of imperilled persons found their parents (primarily the mothers) preferred the punishing educational style, and they found that the lack of supportive educational style was also typical to them however they felt the mother more supportive.

In all scales of the Parental Bonding Instrument firmly significant deviations were found between the two groups. In the case of the group of imperilled persons we found that the parental treatment was characterised by maternal and paternal affection and care, and a lower level of restriction alike, as well as by an intensive maternal and paternal overprotection. Examining the sexes separately the same deviations were revealed in the case of females, however for the males we found significant differences between the two groups only for the lack of paternal affection and care.

During the analysis of the protective factors significant deviations were found between the two inspected groups on several scales of the Family Socialisation and Parental Bonding Instrument. These are demonstrated in table 2 below (only those scales have been included in the table in the case of which significant differences were revealed between the two groups).

Table 2. Descriptive and Comparative Statistics of the results achieved by the increased and normal depression level groups in the Family Socialisation and Parental Bonding Instrument

Family Socialisation Questionnaire	Imperilled group			Imperilled females			Imperilled males		
	Normal depression level	Increased depression level	P<	Normal depression level	Increased depression level	P<	Normal depression level	Increased depression level	P<
Conflict oriented family atmosphere	M=12,3 SD=5,2	M=14,6 SD=6	0,002	M=12,8 SD=5,7	M=14,3 SD=5,9	n. s.	M=11,5 SD=4,3	M=15,7 SD=6,1	0,001
Manipulative educational attitude	M=11 SD=5,6	M=13,2 SD=6,6	0,007	M=10,5 SD=5,9	M=12,8 SD=6,5	0,020	M=11,8 SD=5,2	M=14,4 SD=7,1	n. s.
Conformity as breeding target	M=22 SD=9,1	M=24,6 SD=9	0,031	M=21,5 SD=8,9	M=23,7 SD=9,2	n. s.	M=22,7 SD=9,4	M=27,5 SD=7,5	0,024
Supportive educational style	M=28,4 SD=7	M=26,5 SD=9	0,040	M=29,2 SD=6,3	M=26,3 SD=7	0,008	M=27,1 SD=7,9	M=27,1 SD=6,2	n. s.
Punishing educational style	M=16,5 SD=5,7	M=18,2 SD=6,8	0,016	M=16,6 SD=5,9	M=18,4 SD=7	0,046	M=16,3 SD=5,2	M=17,4 SD=3,8	n. s.
Inconsistent educational attitude	M=6,8 SD=3,8	M=9,3 SD=4,9	0,000	M=6,8 SD=3,5	M=9,6 SD=5	0,000	M=6,8 SD=4,2	M=8,5 SD=4,5	n. s.
Difference between parental family socialisation effects	M=12,5 SD=11,7	M=16,9 SD=13,5	0,014	M=11,7 SD=12	M=16,5 SD=12,1	0,022	M=13,8 SD=11	M=18,5 SD=17	n. s.
Paternal affection-care	M=26,3 SD=7,5	M=22,6 SD=10,5	0,005	M=27 SD=7,4	M=22,5 SD=10,6	0,006	M=25,2 SD=7,6	M=23 SD=10	n. s.
Paternal overprotection	M=3,6 SD=3,8	M=5,6 SD=5	0,002	M=4,1 SD=4,4	M=6 SD=5	0,014	M=2,8 SD=2,6	M=4,2 SD=4,7	n. s.
Paternal restriction	M=11,4 SD=4	M=9,8 SD=4,8	0,010	M=11 SD=4,2	M=9,3 SD=4,7	0,023	M=12,1 SD=3,5	M=11,3 SD=5	n. s.

M=mean value, SD=standard deviation, P= probability for exceeding, n.s.= not significant.

Regarding family atmosphere, considerable differences were revealed for the whole sample concerning the conflict-oriented family atmosphere. The members belonging to the group of increased depression level found that their families were conflict burden. This perception was more intensive in the case of men, but the same did not reach a significant level in the case of women.

Considering the sample as a whole, remarkable differences were revealed between the groups in respect of the breeding targets, namely in breeding to conformity. The men in the increased depression level group perceived that their parents bred them much more to conformity, than those belonging to the other group. This tendency was also observed in the case of women however it did not reach a significant level.

Examining the educational attitudes of parents we found that the groups were significantly different with regard to manipulative and inconsistent educational attitudes considering the whole group. Both educational attitudes were more typical to that of the parents belonging to the members of the increased depression level group. Regarding the manipulative educational attitude we found that in both groups the mother was perceived by the persons to have been more manipulative. Regarding the sex we could confirm same finding only for women. In the case of men the differences between the two groups did not reach the significant level.

With respect to the educational style of parents there was a significant difference found between the groups for both educational styles. While the punishing educational style was typical of the parents in the increased depression level group, the parents of the normal depression level group had a more supportive educational style. Considering the sexes we could confirm the above statement only in the case of women. This tendency was also present in the case of men, but not at a significant level.

Examining the homogeneity of the effects of the parental educational styles we summarised on each family socialisation scale the differences between the maternal and paternal educational styles. We found that the parents of the members belonging to the increased level depression group were much more significantly characterised by the heterogeneity of the effects of parental breeding, than the parents in the other group (t=2.475, p<0.014). In this respect we inspected each scale of Family Socialisation Questionnaire separately as well. We found considerable differences with respect to inconsistent (t=2.796, p<0.006) and consistent (t=2.007, p<0.0046) educational attitudes. The heterogeneity in the effects of the parental breeding here also appeared in the increased depression level group.

Examining the parental treatment no significant difference was found between the two groups in terms of maternal treatment, neither in the case of women nor in the case of men. The members of the increased depression level group regardless of sex found that the mother was less restrictive, giving less affection and care, but being more overprotective. These differences however did not reach the significant level. However in the case of paternal treatment, we managed to detect considerable differences. Considering the sample as a whole and the women in the increased level depression group found that their fathers were significantly less restrictive, giving less affection and care, but overprotective, than the members of the other group. We observed the same tendency for men as well, however in their case it did not reach a significant level.

4. DISCUSSION

Our survey verified in a non-clinical sample (college students) that certain family socialisation factors may play a role as risk and protective factors in the development of depression in the case of vulnerable persons.

First we evaluated the results of our research considering the sample as a whole. Examining the family atmosphere we could identify the conflict burden family atmosphere as a risk factor in line with the results of the researches carried out by Formoso et al., [12], and we managed to prove the protective effect of the calm and conflict free family atmosphere.

From among the breeding targets neither the lack of breeding for autonomy nor the breeding for conformity were revealed as risk factors. As a protective factor, however, we managed to identify the lack of breeding for conformity.

The examination of the parental educational style showed that the punishing educational style can be identified as a risk factor, that certified the results of the researches implemented by Richter [13] Csorba and Hári [14]. Additionally we found that the lack of supportive educational style may also be considered as a risk factor. The opponent end points of this educational style have protective values, that is, the lack of punishing educational style and the preference of supportive breeding style.

Considering the educational attitudes, all three (manipulative, inconsistent, consistent) may emerge as risk factors during family socialisation, if the parents prefer these. The preference of manipulative educational attitude by the parents supports Adler's theory on the development of depression, namely that the depressive behaviour is a subconscious manipulative attempt for the satisfaction of emotional claims (support, empathy and help) [24]. Consistent educational attitude coupled with the punishing educational style may appear as an intensive risk factor. Examining the educational attitudes with respect to the protective effect the lack of manipulative and inconsistent breeding attitudes may have a protective effect.

The results of our research indicate that the homogeneous breeding manner of parents may also appear as a protective effect.

Examining the parental treatment, the lack of maternal and paternal affection and care, as well as the lack of restriction, and the maternal and paternal overprotection may also appear as risk factors. Curiously enough, we did not manage to indicate the protective effect of maternal affection and care when examining the parental treatment. The results of the survey demonstrate that paternal affection, care and restrictions, and the lack of paternal overprotection have protective effect against the development of depression. It seems that the lack of maternal affection and care and the maternal overprotection influence the development of depression only as risk factors, while in the case of the father depending on the lack or existence of the mentioned attitudes they may either be risk factors or have protective impacts.

Examining the results of the researches with regard to sexes we found that in the case of women all the aforementioned risk factors activate their effects. The protective effect of the abovementioned protective factors were also indicated in their cases, except for calm family atmosphere, and the lack of the endeavour of parents to conformity. In the case of men the situation was different. In their case only the conflict burden family atmosphere, the manipulative and inconsistent educational attitude of parents as well as the lack of paternal affection and care appeared as risk factors. The rest of the examined family socialisation factors did not appear in their cases as risk factors. With respect to protective factors the situation was similar. In their case only calm family atmosphere and the lack of the parents' endeavour to conformity had provable protective effects.

The results of our survey indicate that women are more sensitive to the effects of family socialisation appearing as risk and protective factors alike.

The mental hygienic interpretation of the results of our research clearly evidence the need of experts to form the consciousness concerning the discovered risk factors during the supporting and therapy work with families, in order to avoid the manifestation of the serious form of depression requiring clinical treatment in the case of as many persons exposed to risks (imperilled persons) as possible.

REFERENCES

[1]   Brown G.W., & Harris, T., (1986). Establishing Causal Links, The Bedford College Studies of Depression. In Kasching H. (Ed.), *Life Events and Psychiatric Disorders.* London-Cambridge: Univ. Press

[2]   Costello, C.G., (1982). Social Factors Associated With Depression: Retrosprective Communiti Study. *Psychological Medicine, 12,* 329-339.

[3]   O'Neil, M.K., & Lancee, W.J., & Stanly, J., & Freeman, J., (1986). Psychosocial Factors and Depressive Symtoms. *Journal of Nervous and Mental Diseases, 11,* 15-22.

[4]   Lloyd, C., (1980). Life EventsAs Predisposing Factors. *Archives of General Psychiatry, 37,* 529-535.

[5]   Furukawa, T.A., & Ogura, A., & Hirai, T., & Fujihara, S., & Kitamura, T., & Takahasi, K., (1999). Early Parental Seperation ExperiencesAmong Patients With Bipolar Disorder and Major Depression: Case Control Study. *Journal of Affective Disorders, 54,* 85-91.

[6]   Palosaari, U.K., & Aro, H.M., (1999). Parental divorce, self esteem and depression. An intimate relationship as a protective factor in young adulthood. *Journal of Affective Disorders, 35,* 91-96.

[7]   Margitics, F. (2005). Prediszponáló tényezők kapcsolata a szubklinikus depressziós tünetegyüttessel főiskolai hallgatóknál. [Interrelation between predisposition factors and sub clinical depression syndrome at college students.] *Psychiatria Hungarica, 20,* 211-223.

[8]   Aszmann, A., (2001). Fiatalok egészségi állapota és egészségmagatartása. [Health condition and health preservation of the youth.] Budapest: Országos Tisztiorvosi Hivatal.

[9]   Pikó, B., & Fitzpatrick, K.M., (2001). Does class matter? SES and psychosocial health among Hungarian adolescents. *Social Science and Medicine, 53,* 817-830.

[10] Lempers, J.D., & Clark-Lempers, D., (1990). Family economic stress, maternal and paternal support and adolescent distress. *Journal of Adolescence, 13,* 217-229.

[11] Csorba, J., & Dinya, E., & Párt, S., & Solymos, J., (1994): Életesemény kutatás és serdülőkor. A középiskolás életesemény kérdőív bemutatása. [Life event research and

adolescence. The Hungarian version of the Junior High Life Experiences Survey.] *Magyar Pszichológiai Szemle, 50*, 67-83.

[12] Formoso, D., & Gonzales, N.A., & Aiken, L.S., (2000). Family conflict and children's internalizing and externalizing behavior: protective factors. *Am. J. Commun. Psycho, 28*, 175-199.

[13] Richter, J., (1986). Die Erfassung psychosozialer Bezihungen im Jugendalter. *Psych. Praxi, 1*, 63-74.

[14] Csorba, J., & Hári, I., (1995). Életesemények vizsgálata serdülőkori szorongásos kórképekben. [Examination of life events in anxiety disorder syndromes in the case of adolescents.] *Gyermekgyógyászat, 46*, 133-139.

[15] Pikó, B., & Fitzpatrick, K.M., (2001). A rizikó és protektív elmélet alkalmazása a serdülőkori depressziós tünetegyüttes magatartás-epidemiológiai vizsgálatában. [Application of the Risk and Protective Theories in the Behaviour-Epidemiologic Examination of Depressive Syndromes at Adolescent Age.] *Mentálhigiéné és Pszichoszomatika*, 41-47.

[16] Fitzpatrick, K.M., (1997). Fighting among Americ's youth: a risk and protective factors approach. *Journal of Health and Social Behavior, 38*, 131-148.

[17] Dekovic, M., (1999). Risk and protective factors in the development of problem behavior during adolescence. *Journal of Youth and Adolescence, 28*, 667-685.

[18] Beck, A.T., & Beck, R. W. (1972). Screening depressed patients in family practice. A rapid technique. *Postgraduate Medicine, 52*, 81-85.

[19] Goch, I. (1998). *Entwicklung der Ungewissheitstoleranz. Die Bedeutung der familialen Socialization.* Regensburg: Roderer.

[20] Sallay, H., & Dabert, C. (2002). Women's perception of parenting: a German-Hungarian comparison. *Applied Psychology in Hungary, 3-4*, 55-56.

[21] Sallay, H., & Krotos, H. (2004). Az igazságos világba vetett hit fejlődése: japán és magyar kultúrközi összehasonlítás. [Evolution of belief in a fair world: Japanese and Hungarian intercultural comparison.] *Pszichológia, 24*, 233—252.

[22] Parker, G., & Tupling, H., & Brown, L. B. (1979). A Parental Bonding Instrument. *British Journal of Medicinal Psychiatry, 52*, 1-10.

[23] Tóth, I., & Gervai, J. (1999). Szülői Bánásmód Kérdőív (H-PBI): a Parental Bonding Instrument magyar változata. [Perceived parental styles: the Hungarian version of the Parental Bonding Instrument (H-PBI).] *Magyar Pszichológiai Szemle, 54*, 551-566.

[24] Adler, A., (1937). *Emberismeret. Gyakorlati individuálpszichológia (Practical individual psychology).* Budapest: Rekord Publishing Company.

Chapter 5

GENDER DIFFERENCES IN PRONENESS TO DEPRESSION AMONG COLLEGE STUDENTS

ABSTRACT

Our research aimed to find out what role the risk mechanisms, as described in Goodman and Gotlib's (1999) model (genetic-biological, interpersonal, social learning related cognitive and stress related factors), play in the development of increased risk for depression in the case of men and women. The genetic-biological factors were examined with certain temperament characteristics, the interpersonal factors with parental educational purpose, educational attitudes, educational style and parental treatment. In the case of factors related to social learning we looked at the dysfunctional attitudes and the attributional style. As far as the stressors are concerned, we observed the quality of family atmosphere, and the number of the positive and negative life events of the preceding six months and their subjective evaluation. 681 students took part in the research (465 women and 216 men). Our research results show that all of the increased risk mechanisms, namely the genetic-biological, interpersonal, social learning related cognitive, and stress related factors are connected with the development of liability to depression, explaining 41.4% of the depression symptoms' variance in the case of women, and 36.5% in the case of men. Harm avoidance, a genetic-biological factor, proved to be the most significant risk mechanism, irrespective of the sexes. From among the environmental factors – irrespective of the sexes - one stress related factor, the subjective evaluation of negative life experiences, which implies an increased sensitivity to stress, proved to be the strongest risk mechanism. While the above factors played an important role in the development of vulnerability to depression in both sexes, the social learning related cognitive and interpersonal risk mechanisms differed in their degree in women and men. In the case of women the social learning related mechanisms proved to be stronger and higher impact risk factors than in the case of men. The effect of interpersonal factors seemed to be relatively the weakest in the development of increased risk for depression.

1. INTRODUCTION

Several well-documented studies carried out in the field of psychiatric epidemiology have proved a higher prevalence of depression among women. A great number of studies have dealt with the differences between the genders in the cases of chronic minor depression and dysthymia [1]. These studies consistently found that the proportion of prevalence is 2:1. Kessler et al. [2], in minor depression, Angst and Merikangas [1] in short repetitive depression, found a consistently higher prevalence among women than among men. On the other hand, they did not find major differences between the genders in the prevalence of mania, neither in epidemiological research [3], nor in clinical studies [4].

The question arises of whether the proportion of prevalence is the same between the genders if the age of the study population is examined as well. Kessler at al. [5] compared a retrospective age-of-onset reports in a representative cross-sectional research with reports across subsamples of different age respondents. Group scales gained after the study of data distribution showed that differences between the genders relating to depression surfaced at the age of 11-15 and remained consistently higher later on.

Over the years several theories have been made to explain these differences between the genders. For instance, the female role theories argue that chronic stress connected to traditional female roles may cause higher prevalence of depression among women [6]. According to the rumination theory, women are more likely to deal with a problem longer than men and, as a result, the temporary symptoms of disphory turn to major parts of depression [7]. Both perspectives assume that the higher prevalence of clinically more significant depression among women is, at least partly, the result of their higher persistence.

Goodman and Gotlib [8] suggest the separation of four mechanisms within an integrative model with the help of which the increased risk for depression can be explained. Two of these mechanisms are primarily genetical-biological while the other two are cognitive-interpersonal: the first mechanism focuses on the genetic factors, on the heritability of depression, the second is connected to innate dysfunctional neuroregulatory mechanisms, the third mechanism focuses on the confused interpersonal relations and dysfunctional cognitions related to social learning, the fourth mechanism includes the stressful context of a child's life; thus it can be connected to the stress load of a child

According to Goodman and Gotlib [8], all four abovementioned mechanisms are possible mechanisms of the increased risk for depression, but it is not quite clear to what extent they are responsible for the development of risk, or furthermore how they interact with each other. It is possible that one or more are present at the same time.

A substantial amount of literature discusses the consistent genetic transmission of depressive disturbance in the case of adults. According to the studies, which examined twins, families and adopted people, the risk for depression in the case of first grade relatives of those suffering from affective disturbance is 20-25%, in contrast to the 7% of risk level among the average population [9]. The genetic analysis of behaviour has proved numerous correlations with the high possibility of inheritance for depression [10]. Among other factors, temperament [11], behavioral inhibition and timidity [12], neuroticism [13] and sociability [14] may increase vulnerability to depression and be special factors in connection with inheritance. The results of modern temperament studies indicate that a tendency to avoid harm may be considered as the basic factor of biological vulnerability to depression which appears as a characteristic feature as early as in childhood. Harm avoidance refers to an inherited pattern which may appear in the form of passive avoidance and fear of the uncertain [15]. According to studies carried out by Hansen et al. [16], harm avoidance and low self-directedness are in harmony with the degree of depression.

A great number of studies have examined the connection between interpersonal factors and depression. In his studies, Parker [17] noted that those suffering from neurotic depression had received less parental attention, and higher maternal overprotection. In non-clinic groups the signs of depression were also related to less parental attention, and showed a slight correlation with parental overprotection. According to Parker's [18] research results, the correlation between lower parental care and depression was independent of the degree of depression. In his later studies Parker [19] argued that the kind of parental care which is characterised by low attention and high overprotection is linked to the high risk of neurotic disturbance (depressive neurosis, social phobia, anxiety neurosis), while the additional risk for psychotic disturbance is low or completely non-existent. In research carried out by Mackinnon and his colleagues [20] on non-clinic samples, lack of parental care was the number one risk factor of depression, as opposed to overprotection. Narita and his colleagues [21] carried out a study of Japanese samples and found that low parental care was always connected with depression at any age and the connection between depression and overprotection was obvious, also.

Problematic parental care related to cognitive functions and styles may have a negative effect on children's development. Dysfunctional attitudes may have a significant role in the development of depression. The unbalanced gradation of these attitudes with abilities and possibilities may also lead to the development of symptoms of depression. If a person has high expectations of himself and his surroundings in many fields of life, and is not able to meet the expectations of his context, he may then easily have a negative self-evaluation which can directly lead to hopelessness, which in turn can cause the development of symptoms of depression [22]. According to Beck, those characterised with dysfunctional attitudes are more likely to develop depression. These attitudes may not automatically cause illness when they are present separately. Furthermore, some of these insets might be an important drive in society, but their accumulation or high level may create a tendency for pathological development [23].

In Garber's and Hilsman's [24] cognitive diathesis-stress model, in addition to dysfunctional attitudes, another cognitive factor, the negative attributional style, may also play a key role in the appearance of depressive symptoms. It is assumed that copying significant others, parental refusal and uncontrollable stressful events may be responsible for the development of the negative cognitive style. According to Metalsky, Halberstadt and Abramson's studies [25], students with a negative, pessimistic attributive style were more distressed than those who had a more optimistic attributive style. According to Peterson et al. [26], this negative attributional style is connected to physical illnesses; people who can be described with this attributional style do not care about themselves and their negative lifestyle may lead to illness. According to Abramson, Metalsky and Alloy [27], the pessimistic attributional style alone is not an adequate cause of depression. It becomes important when the individual encounters strong or frequent negative events. In their opinion, in the development of depression the extent a person believes his life can be influenced is more important than how he interprets unpleasant events. The belief that he is able to tackle problems increases his resistance to depression.

Those who have suffered from depression are more vulnerable to stressful life events than those who do not have such a history of depression. According to Brown and Harris' vulnerability theory, depression occurs in an interaction between the individual and his environment. The joint appearance and interaction of predispositional factors and external events (provoking factors) are needed for its evolvement. Predispositional factors can be certain personality characteristics (self-evaluation, self-power, conflict solving strategies, degree of distress endurance, relationship ability, etc.), traumatic family prehistory, disturbed personality development, and the deficiency of the social criteria system. Life events work as provoking factors, and external events, as stressors, contribute to the manifestation of depression. However, the interpretation of life events is unique, and it depends on the antecedents of personality development. Negative life events do not cause depression, but they may contribute to the development of depression.

The aim of this paper is to find out what role the risk mechanisms, as described in Goodman and Gotlib's [8] model (genetical-biological, interpersonal, social learning related cognitive and stress related factors), have in the development of increased risk for depression in the case of men and women. (Due to methodological difficulties we left out the innate dysfunctional neuroregulatory risk-transfer mechanisms.) The genetical-biological factors were examined with certain temperament characteristics, the interpersonal factors with parental educational purpose, educational attitudes, educational style and parental treatment. In the case of factors related to social learning we looked at dysfunctional attitudes and attribution style. As far as stressors are concerned, we observed the quality of family atmosphere, and the number of positive and negative life events of the preceding six months and their subjective evaluation.

2. METHOD

Participants

Data was collected among college students at the College of Nyíregyháza, in a county seat in the north-eastern part of Hungary. We collected data randomly at every faculty and participation was voluntary and it was done with their consent. Students filled out the questionnaires individually at lectures with the guidance of the researchers.

700 students took part in the research and 681 of them provided valuable data (465 female and 216 male). According to their majors, the following students participated in the study: 225 undergraduate BA students, 125 undergraduate BSc students, 125 business students, 74 students studying to be infant teachers, 70 studying to be social studies teachers and 62 students of arts (visual arts and music).

The average age was 19.98 (standard deviation 1.51) the median value was 20 years.

Measures

To study depression we applied an abridged version of the 13 item multiple-choice questionnaire of the Beck Depression Inventory [30, 31]. The inventory studies the following components of depressive syndromes: sadness, pessimism, sense of failure, dissatisfaction, guilt, fear of punishment, self-harm, indecisiveness, social withdrawal, self-image change, work difficulty, fatigability and anorexia.

To study genetical-biological factors we applied the Hungarian version of Cloninger's Temperament and Character Inventory adapted by Rózsa and his colleagues [15]. The temperament dimension measuring scales of the questionnaire were the following: novelty seeking, harm avoidance, reward dependence and persistence.

To study interpersonal factors (effects of family socialisation) we applied the Goch's Family Socialisation Questionnaire [32, 33]. The following scales of the questionnaire were used in the study: maternal educational aims (independence – autonomy, as an educational aim; conformity – conformity as an educational aim), maternal educational attitudes (consistent, manipulative or inconsistent attitude) and maternal educational style (supportive or punitive style).

To study interpersonal factors we applied the Hungarian adaptation of Parker and his colleagues' questionnaire on Parental Treatment [34]. The following dimensions of parental treatment were examined: maternal care, maternal overprotection, maternal control, paternal care, paternal overprotection and paternal control.

The study of cognitive factors related to social learning: We used the Hungarian adaptation of Weismann's Dysfunctional Attitude Scale to examine dysfunctional attitudes [35, 36]. The questionnaire examines the following attitudes: need for external recognition, need to be loved, need for achievement, perfectionism, rightful increased expectations towards context, omnipotence (increased altruism orientation), external control –autonomy.

The attributive style was examined by using Abramson and his colleagues' Attributional Style Questionnaire [37]. The attributive style was valued on the following factors: internal or external attribution, stable or instable attribution, specific or global attribution. The research participants were asked to form judgements about the following situations: judgment of performance (exam failure) and judgment of loss (breaking up a relationship with a close friend).

To study stressors we applied the Goch's Family Socialisation Questionnaire [32, 33]. The following scale of the questionnaire was used in the research: the type of family atmosphere (conflict-oriented family atmosphere).

To study stressors we applied the High School Life Experience Questionnaire of Cohen and his colleagues, adapted by Csorba and his colleagues for the Hungarian context [38].The questionnaire focused on the frequent, mainly negative, but sometimes partly positive, life events of the preceding six months. The questionnaire measured the following dimensions: number of positive life events, score of positive life events, number of negative life events, score of negative life events.

3. RESULTS

The Connection between Genetical-Biological
Factors and Depression

The presence of biological vulnerability was examined by the use of Cloninger's Temperament and Character Inventory. Linear regression analysis was used in observing the relationship between certain temperament scales (novelty seeking, harm avoidance, reward dependence, persistence) as independent variables, and the values measured by Beck's Depression Inventory, as dependent variables.

Table 1. summarizes the connection between depression and certain temperament scales of the different sexes.

Table 1. The regression of depression on genetical-biological factors

Predictor	β	t	p<
Women: Ftotal=73.670; p<0.000			
Harm avoidance	0.511	12.124	0.000
Novelty seeking	0.165	3.910	0.000
Men: Ftotal=30.994; p<0.000			
Harm avoidance	0.431	7.099	0.000
Reward dependence	-0.158	-2.543	0.012

In both sexes, about the same proportion of depression variance is explained by the genetic-biological factors (24.2% of women, 22.5% of men). In both sexes, we have found a very tight connection between depression and harm avoidance. Harm avoiding people are more likely to be pessimistic, careful, timid, stressed, distressed, afraid of danger, risks, tend to be worried, reserved, hampered and are easily exhausted [15]. Furthermore, in the case of women, novelty seeking had a positive correlation with depression. Novelty seekers are impulsive, and they are open to new things, but lose their patience easily. They are irresolute, they quickly get bored with what they are doing, they are irritable and unstable. Extravagant behaviour, lack of restraint and untidiness may also characterise them [15]. In the case of men, reward dependence had a significant negative correlation with depression. Less reward dependent people are indifferent to social signals, and are more liable to being socially isolated, emotionally cold and pragmatic [15].

The Connection between Interpersonal Factors and Depression

As far as interpersonal factors were concerned, we were primarily interested in the role of parents in the family socialisation process. Among the effects of family socialisation we focused on the parent's educational aims (education for self-sufficiency - autonomy as an educational aim, education for conformity – conformity as an educational aim), educational attitudes (consistent educational attitude, manipulative educational attitude, and inconsistent educational attitude), educational styles (supportive style, punitive style), and parental treatment (care, overprotection and control). With linear regression analysis we examined the connection between the abovementioned variables, as independent variables, and the values measured by Beck's Depression Inventory, as dependent variables.

Table 2. shows the connection between depression and certain interpersonal factors of the sexes.

**Table 2. The regression of depression
on certain interpersonal factors**

Predictor	β	T	p<
Women: Ftotal=19.944; p<0.000			
Parents' manipulative educational attitude	0.188	3.734	0.000
Paternal care	-0.156	-3.273	0.001
Maternal control	-0.134	-2.974	0.003
Parents' inconsistent educational attitude	0.108	2.020	0.044
Men: Ftotal=12.615; p<0.000			
Paternal care	-0.204	-2.733	0.007
Parents' inconsistent educational attitude	0.186	2.493	0.013

The interpersonal factors explain nearly the same rate the variance of depression in both sexes. Though in the case of women, the rate is somewhat higher (15.3 %) than in the case of men (11.1 %). In both cases depression was closely connected to the parents' inconsistent educational attitude and the lack of paternal care. In the case of women, the parents' manipulative attitude and the lack of maternal care also contributed to the risk of developing depression.

The Connection between Depression and Social Learning Related Cognitive Factors

From the cognitive factors related to depression, we examined dysfunctional attitudes (need for acknowledgement, love, achievement, perfectionism, rightfully increased expectations towards the context, omnipotence, external control – autonomy) and the attributional style (internal or external, stable or unstable, specific or global attribution). With the help of linear regression analysis we examined the connection between the above mentioned variables, as independent variables, and values measured by Beck's Depression Inventory, as dependent variables.

Table 3 shows the connection between depression and certain social learning factors of the sexes.

**Table 3. The regression of depression
on certain social learning factors**

Predictor	β	t	p<
Women: Ftotal=45.717; p<0.000			
External control-autonomy	0.289	6.920	0.000
Performance: specific or global	0.256	6.079	0.000
Performance: stable or instable	0.161	3.841	0.001
Men: Ftotal=11.402; p<0.000			
External control-autonomy	0.213	3.282	0.000
Loss: specific or global	0.173	2.538	0.012
Performance: specific or global	0.163	2.258	0.019

In the case of women, the cognitive factors related to social learning explained a greater variance of depression than in the case of men (women: 22.5 %, men: 12.8 %). In both sexes, among the dysfunctional attitudes, depression showed a close connection with external control attitude. A person with external control attitudes feels he does not have control over his life, instead things just happen to him. While examining the attributional styles we found that women perceive the causes of losing control over their judgment of performance deficit as stable ("it will always be that way") and global, such that has an effect on every aspect of their life. Men, on the other hand, see the cause of both control loss and performance deficit as global.

The Connection between Depression and Stress Related Factors

When examining the connection between stress and depression we looked at the quality of family atmosphere (its conflict load on the individual's life up to the time of investigation) and the number of positive and negative life events in the preceding six months and their subjective evaluation (the degree of positive or negative effect). With the help of linear regression analysis, we examined the connection between the abovementioned variables as independent variables, and values measured by Beck's Depression Inventory, as dependent variables.

Table 4 shows the connection between depression and certain stress related factors of the sexes.

Table 4. The regression of depression on certain stress related factors

Predictor	β	t	p<
Women: Ftotal=63.668; p<0.000			
Evaluation of negative life events	0.374	8.689	0.000
Conflict oriented family atmosphere	0.188	4.358	0.000
Men: Ftotal=17.658; p<0.000			
Evaluation of negative life events	0.331	4.772	0.017
Conflict oriented family atmosphere	0.170	2.494	0.013

In the case of women, stress related factors explained a greater variance of depression (women: 21.6%, men: 14.2%). In both sexes depression was closely, significantly connected to both the subjective evaluation of negative life experiences in the preceding six months, and the conflict-oriented family atmosphere.

The Role of the Examined Factors in the Development of Depression

In the following model we included all those variables which showed a strong correlation with depression when examining the different factors (table 5).

The result of regression analysis shows that in the case of women the examined risk mechanisms explained a greater variance of depression than in the case of men (women: 41.4%, men: 36.5%).

The genetic-biological factors of risk mechanisms were stronger in the case of men, since two temperament factors, harm avoidance and reward dependence, proved to be greater risk factors. In the case of women this was only true for harm avoidance.

The interpersonal factors as risk mechanisms did not prove a significant correlation with depression. In the case of women, only the inconsistent parental educational attitude, while in the case of men, the lack of paternal care proved to be risk factors.

Out of the social learning related cognitive factors, one of the negative attributional styles, the experience of control loss as stable ("it will always be that way") proved to be a great risk factor. This acted as a distorting factor for women when judging performance deficit and it had the same effect for men when judging loss. Furthermore, in the case of women we were able to prove the role of another social learning related risk factor, the external control attitude.

Out of the stress related factors, only the subjective evaluation of negative life experiences proved to be a risk factor.

Table 5. The regression of depression on those variables
which had a strong correlation with depression during the research

Predictor	β	t	p<
Women: F_{total}=61.561; p<0.000			
Harm avoidance	0.340	8.886	0.000
Evaluation of negative life events	0.244	6.153	0.000
Performance: specific or global	0.166	4.342	
External control-autonomy	0.151	3.831	0.000
Parents' inconsistent educational attitude	0.145	3.806	0.002
Men: F_{total}=25.651; p<0.000			
Harm avoidance	0.365	6.260	0.000+
Evaluation of negative life events	0.267	4.623	0.000
Loss: specific or global	0.158	2.774	
Reward dependence	-0.154	-2.709	0.006
Paternal care	-0.152	-2.602	0.008

4. DISCUSSION

The aim of this present study was to show the differences between the sexes in their predisposition to depression, using a non-clinical sample. We examined what role those factors which are considered increased risk mechanisms (genetic-biological, interpersonal, social learning related cognitive and stress related factor) play in the development of increased risk for depression in women and men.

The results of the study show that all of the increased risk mechanisms, thus the genetical-biological, the interpersonal, the social learning related cognitive and stress related factors, are connected to the development of predisposition to depression and they explain 41.4% of the depression symptoms' variance in the case of women, and 36.5% in the case of men.

According to the results of our study, harm avoidance, a genetic-biological factor, proved to be the most significant risk mechanism, irrespective of the sexes. Cloninger [39] believes that of the temperament factors, harm avoidance is the most important one as it has a control influence on the other two, and it appears first during ontogenesis. Reward dependence, another temperament factor, was also a risk factor for men. It is in harmony with the results of other studies [15] according to which the ability of emotional reaction is generally not affected by depression, only a specific disturbance of emotional reactions to joyful stimuli can be detected, which may be the result of a malfunctioning reward system. Besides these, the other risk mechanisms – interpersonal, cognitive and stress related factors—also have an important role in the development of increased risk to depression in men and women, though to a different degree, higher for women and lower for men. When examining twins, Kendler et al. [40] found that while the development of clinical, major depression was connected primarily to additive genetic factors, the development of milder, sub-clinical forms of depression was influenced mainly by environmental factors. The results of our research, carried out with a non-clinical sample, prove that although harm avoidance, as a genetic-biological factor, showed the strongest correlation with depression symptoms, it was the environmental factors which were more dominant on the whole.

From among the environmental factors – irrespective of the sexes- one stress-related factor, the subjective evaluation of negative life experiences, which implies an increased sensitivity to stress, proved to be the strongest risk mechanism. Nowadays a great number of theorists believe that there are many environmental factors which increase the risk of vulnerability to depression, and that these are inherited. For example, Plomin [41] argues that genetic factors contribute to the difference of variables such as poor parental care or the reaction to stressful life events. In 1978, Brown and Harris [42] already pointed out the fact that sensitivity to stress is genetically transmitted. According to the results of our research, this transmitted factor, which lies behind the harm avoiding behaviour, may be the genetic-biological mechanism. Harm avoidance means the inherited pattern of behavioural inhibition, which may manifest itself in passive avoiding behaviour and in fear of uncertainty. Several studies [15] have pointed out that certain groups of children, even before acquiring social experiences, are more diffident, more uncertain and tense in unknown situations than their peers; they avoid new stimuli, do not adapt easily to changes and their mood is often gloomy and negative. These factors may increase vulnerability to depression by leading children towards choosing or avoiding certain types of environment and making them selectively react to certain aspects of their environment. As a result, the child perceives the world with a bias and reacts more sensitively to environmental stress. This may even be related to the fact that the negative, pessimistic attribution style, a factor related to social learning, also plays a major role in the development of predisposition to depression in both sexes. One of its characteristic marks, the experience of control loss as stable ("it will always be that way"), showed a specific relationship with depression symptoms. This, however, appeared in different areas in the sexes. The relationship was found in the area of achievement in the case of women, while it was detected in the area of loss in the case of men. Joiner and Wagner [43] found moderate proof that the negative attributional style may be a predictor of increasing depressive symptoms in children and adolescents.

While both the genetic-biological and stress-related risk mechanisms played an important role in the development of vulnerability to depression in both sexes, the social learning related cognitive and interpersonal risk mechanisms differed in their degree in women and men. Besides the pessimistic attribution style, the external control attitude – another social learning related risk mechanism – had an important role in the development of increased risk for depression. According to Fiske and Taylor [44], when defining a person's self-evaluation and self-image, the extent the individual considers himself effective in a given situation and how much control and influence he believes he may have over it are very important. Therefore, the perception of control is an important aspect of how an individual behaves in a certain situation. A person with external control attitude feels he does not have control over his life, things just happen to him. The resulting passive, inert state, according to Seligman [45], may develop the implicit belief that he has no control over his life and whatever he does has no impact on the course of actions in his life. This might make him passive, his motivation may decrease and he may be liable to depression.

The effect of interpersonal factors seemed to be relatively the weakest in the development of increased risk for depression. The biological and cognitive factors for liability to depression are formed in the interaction of the personality and the environment, primarily within the social context created by the parents. The dissonance between the child's temperament and the expectations and requirements of the social context may act as a predispositional factor for the development of depression [15]. According to our research findings, such a factor for women can be the inconsistent parental educational attitude, and, in the case of men, the lack of paternal care.

REFERENCES

[1]   Angst, J., & Merikangsamm, K. (1997). The depressive spectrum: Diagnostic classification and course. *Journal of Affective Disorders.* 45, 31-39.

[2]   Kessler, R.C., & Zhao, S., & Blazer, D.G., & Swartz, M.S. (1997). Prevalence, correlates and course of minor depression and major depression in the NCS. *Journal of Affective Disorders.* 45, 19-30.

[3]   Kessler, R.C., & Wittchen, H.U., & Abelson, J.M., & McGonagle, K.A., & Schwarz, N., & Kendler, K.S. et al. (1998). Methodological studies of the Composite International Diagnostic Interview (CIDI) in the US National Comorbidity Survey Int. *J. Methods. Psychiatr. Res.* 7, 33-55.

[4]   Goodwin, F.K., & Jamison, K.J. (1990). *Manic-Depressive Illness.* New York, Oxford University Press.

[5]   Kessler, R.C., & McGonagle, K.A., & Nelson C.B., & Hughes M., & Swartz, M.S., & Blazer D.G. (1994). Sex and depression in the National Comorbidity Survey II: Cohort effect. *Journal Affective Disorders.* 30, 15-26.

[6]   Mirowsky, J., & Ross, C.E. (1989). *Social Cases of Psychological Distress.* New York: Aldine De Gruyter.

[7]   Noel-Hoeksema, S. (1990). Sex differences in unipolar depression: Evidence and theory. *Psychological Bulletin.* 101, 259-282.

[8] Goodman, S. H., & Gotlib, I. H. (1999). Risk for psychopathology in the children of depressed mothers: A developmental model for understanding mechanisms of transmission. *Psychological Review.* 3, 458-490.

[9] Tsuang, M.T., & Faraone, S.V. (1990). *The genetics of mood disorders.* Baltimore: John Hopkins University Press.

[10] Loehlin, J.C. (1992). *Genes and environment in personality development.* Beverly Hills, CA: Sage.

[11] Goldschmith, H.H., & Buss, K.A., & Lemery, K.S. (1997). Toddler and childhood temperament: Expanded content, stronger genetic evidence, new evidence for the importance of environment. *Developmental Psychology.* 33, 891-905.

[12] Cherny, S.S., & Fulker, D.W., & Corley, R.P., & Plomin, R., & DeFries, J.C. (1994). Continuity and change in infant shyness from 14 to 20 months. *Behavior Genetics.* 24, 365-379.

[13] Tellegen, A., & Lykken, D.T., & Bouchard, T.J., & Wilcox, K.J., & Segal, N.L., & Rich, S. (1988). Personality similarity in twins reared apart and together. *Journal of Personality and Social Psychology.* 54, 1031-1039.

[14] Plomin, R., & Emde, R.N., & Braungart, J.M., & Campos, J., & Corley, R., & Fulk, D.W. et al. (1993). Genetic change and continuity from fourteen twenty months: The MacArthur Longitudinal Twin Study. *Child Development.* 64, 1354-1376.

[15] Rózsa S., & Kállai, J., & Osváth, A., & Bánki M. Cs. (2005). Temperamentum és karakter: Cloninger pszichobiológiai modellje. A Cloninger-féle temperamentum és karakter kérdőív felhasználói kézikönyve. [Temperament and character. Cloninger's psychobiologycal model. The handbook of the Cloninger Temperament and Character Inventory.] Budapest: Medicina Könyvkiadó Rt.

[16] Hansenne, M., & Reggers, J., & Pinto, M., & Kjiri, K., and Ajamier, A., & Ansseau, M. (1999). Temperament and character inventory and depression. *Journal of Psychiatric Research.* 33, 31-36.

[17] Parker, G. (1979). Parenthal characteristics in relation to depressive disorders. *British Journal of Psychiatry.* 134, 138-147.

[18] Parker, G. (1981). Parental representations of patients with anxiety neurosis. *Acta Psychiatrica Scandinavica.* 63, 33-36.

[19] Parker, G. (1983). Parental „affectionless control" as an antecedent to adult depression. A risk factor delineated. *Archives of General Psychiatry.* 40, 956-960.

[20] Mackinnon, A.J., & Henderson, A.S., & Andrews, G. (1993). Parental, affectionless control" as an antecedent to adult depression: a risk factor refined. *Psychological Medicine.* 23, 135-141.

[21] Narita, T., & Sato, T., & Hirano, S., & Gota, M., & Sakado, K., & Uehara, T. (2000). Parental child-rearing behavior as measured the Parental Bonding Instrument in a Japanese population: factor structure and relationship to a lifetime history of depression. *Journal of Affective Disorders.* 57, 229-234.

[22] Kopp, M., & Skrabski, Á. (1995). Alkalmazott magatartástudomány. [Applied science of behavior.] Budapest: Corvinus Kiadó.

[23] Beck, Á.T., & Rush, A.J, & Shaw, B.F., & Emery, G. (2001). A depresszió kognitív terápiája. [The cognitive therapy of depression.] Budapest: Animula.

[24] Garber, J., & Hilsram R. (1992). Cognition, stress, and depression in children and adolescents. *Child and Adolescent Psychiatric Clinics of North America.* 1, 129-167.

[25] Metalsky, G.I., & Halberstadt, L.J., & Abramson, L.Y. (1987). Vulnerability to depressive mood reactions. *Journal of Personality and Social Psychology*. 52, 386-393.

[26] Peterson, C., & Semmel, A., & von Baeyer, C., & Abramson, L.Y., & Metalsky, G.I., & Seligman, M.E.P. (1982). The Attributional Style Questionnaire. *Cognitive Therapy and Research*. 6, 287-299.

[27] Abramson, L Y., & Metalsky, G.I., & Alloy, L.B. (1989). Hopelessness depression: a theory –based subtype of depression. *Psychological Review*. 96, 358-372.

[28] Brown, G.W., & Harris, T. (1986). Establishing Causal Links, The Bedford College Studies of Depression. In H. Kasching (Ed.), *Life Events and Psychiatric Disorders*. (pp.125-129). London-Cambridge: University Press.

[29] Kessler, R.C., & Magee, W.J. (1993). Childhood adversities and adult depression: Basic patterns of association in a US National Survey. *Psychological Medicine*. 23, 679-690.

[30] Beck, A.T., & Beck R.W. (1972). Screening depressed patients in family practice. A rapid technique. *Postgraduate Medicine*. 52, 81-85.

[31] Margitics, F. (2005). Prediszponáló tényezők kapcsolata a szubklinikus depressziós tünetegyüttessel főiskolai hallgatóknál. [Interrelation between predisposition factors and sub clinical depression syndrome at college students.] *Psychiatria Hungarica*. 20, 211-223.

[32] Goch, I. (1998). Entwicklung der Ungewissheitstoleranz. Die Bedeutung der familialen Socialization. Regensburg: Roderer.

[33] Sallay, H., & Dabert, C. (2002). Women's perception of parenting: a German-Hungarian comparison. *Applied Psychology in Hungary*. 3-4, 55-56.

[34] Tóth, I., & Gervai, J. (1999). Szülői Bánásmód Kérdőív (H-PBI): a Parental Bonding Instrument magyar változata. [Perceived parental styles: the Hungarian version of the Parental Bonding Instrument (H-PBI).] *Magyar Pszichológiai Szemle*. 54, 551-566.

[35] Weismann, A.N., & Beck, A.T. (1979). The Dysfunctional Attitude Scale. Thesis, University of Pennsylvania.

[36] Kopp, M. (1994). Orvosi pszichológia. [Medical psychology.] Budapest: SOTE Magatartástudományi Intézet.

[37] Atkinson, R.L., & Atkinson C.R., & Smith E.E., & Bem D.J. (1995). *Pszichológia*. [Psychology.] Budapest: Osiris.

[38] Csorba, J., & Dinya, E., & Párt, S., & Solymos, J. (1994). Életesemény kutatás és serdülőkor. A középiskolás életesemény kérdőív bemutatása. [Life event research and adolescence. The Hungarian version of the Junior High Life Experiences Survey.] *Magyar Pszichológiai Szemle*. 50, 67-83.

[39] Cloninger, C.R. (1987). A systematic method for clinical description and classification of personality variants. *Archives of General Psychiatry*. 44, 573-588.

[40] Kendler K.S., & Kessler R.C., & Walters, E.E., & Maclean, C.J., & Sham P.C., & Neale M.C. et al.(1995). Stressful live evens, genetic liability and onset of an episode of major depression in women. *American Journal of Psychiatry*. 152, 833-842.

[41] Plomin R. (1994). *Genetics and experience: The interplay between nature and nurture*. Thousand Oaks, CA: Sage.

[42] Brown, G.W., & Harris, T. (1978). Social origins of depression. New York: Free press.

[43] Joiner, T.E., & Wagner, K.D. Attributional style and depression in children and adolescents: A meta-analytic review. *Clinical Psychology Review*. 15, 777-789.

[44]   Fiske, S. T., & Taylor S. E. (1984). *Social cognition.* New York, Random House.
[45]   Seligman, M.E.P. (1992). Wednesday's children. *Psychology Today.* 25, 61-67.

Chapter 6

INTERRELATIONS OF TEMPERAMENT AND CHARACTER TYPES WITH SUBCLINICAL DEPRESSION SYNDROMES, DISFUNCTIONAL ATTITUDES AND COPING STRATEGIES OF COLLEGE STUDENTS

ABSTRACT

The objective of this study is to scrutinize the interrelations of the temperament and character types that are separable well by means of the Cloninger's Temperament and Character Inventory (TCI) with the depressive syndromes, dysfunctional attitudes and coping strategies among college students. There were 465 women and 216 men students (n=681) involved in the research. The Temperament and Character Inventory was used for separating the temperament and character types while the abridged version of Beck's Depression Inventory was applied for measuring the rate of depression. The dysfunctional attitudes were determined by the usage of the Hungarian version of Weismann's Dysfunctional Attitude Scale, and the coping strategies were examined through the Hungarian adaptation of Folkman and Lazarus's Conflict Solving Questionnaire. The findings of the studies demonstrated that each temperament and character type could be typified with an individual combination of depressive syndromes, dysfunctional attitudes, and coping strategies. During our surveys we discovered the dysfunctional attitudes and coping strategies being typical of the mature and immature character types.

1. INTRODUCTION

In Cloninger's integrative personality model [1, 2] importance is attached equally to biological and genetic factors as well as learning and social impacts with respect to the development of personality. While congenital elements play a principal role in the evolution of temperament factors, learning and environment have the main effect on character factors. Temperament is characterized by varied automatic responses to emotional stimuli, while the feature of the character is determined by the conception of the self, of others and the world.

Despite the fact that differences that are manifested in temperament factors may be observed already in early infanthood, the evolution of character takes place as the socialisation proceeds, through the social impacts which the individual is exposed to. Temperament and character determines together the entire personality.

According to Cloninger [1, 2] the temperament factors (novelty seeking, harm avoidance and reward-dependence) may be considered to be genetically independent of each other, although they collaborate functionally, they give rise to a wide range of personal answers. Character factors reflect the three stages in self-conception progress. The first stage is the manifestation of individual autonomy (self-directedness); in the second stage personality shows as an integrant of society (collaboration), while the third stage represents the integration with the universe, as the unity of things (transcendence).

Cloninger's theory has distinguished eight temperament and eight character types by virtue of high or low scores given to individual temperament scales (novelty seeking, harm avoidance and reward-dependence) and each character scale (self-directedness, collaboration, transcendence).

The purpose of our research in this case was to scrutinize and reveal the details regarding the individual features of temperament and character types which may be dissociated by means of the world widely applied Cloninger's Temperament and Character Inventory elaborated recently and adapted into Hungarian by Rózsa et al. [2].

In principle, we have intended to examine the correlations that may exist between the individual temperament and character types with the depressive syndromes, dysfunctional attitudes and coping strategies, among college students. With the results of our study we intend to contribute to and assist the work of professionals dealing with the preservation of mental health of the increasing number of university and college students. Our findings are primarily applicable efficiently in the field of consultancy practices and processes.

2. METHOD

Participants

Data was collected among students at the College of Nyíregyháza. We collected data randomly at every faculty and participation was voluntary and it was done with their consent. 700 students took part in the research and 681 of them provided valuable data (465 female and 216 male).

The average age was 19.98 (standard deviation 1.51) the median value was 20 years.

When examining the individual temperament and character types we included the temperament or character type actually under review in the test group and the rest of the sample was placed in the control group.

Measures

The following research methods were used:
Survey of the actual symptoms of depression:

To study depression, we applied the abridged screening version of Beck's Depression Inventory [3, 4].

- The inventory studies the following components of depressive syndromes: sadness, pessimism, sense of failure, dissatisfaction, guilt, fear of punishment, suicide thoughts, indecisiveness, social withdrawal, self-image change, work difficulty, fatigability and anorexia.

Survey of the attitudes:
The Hungarian version of Weismann's Scale of Dysfunctional Attitudes [5, 6] was used.

- The scale included questions about the following attitudes: desire for external appraisal, need for affection, performance orientation, perfectionism, rightful and intensive requirements towards the environment, omnipotence (intensive altruism) and external control - autonomy.

Examination of coping strategies:
The Hungarian adaptation of Lazarus's Conflict Solving Questionnaire [5, 7].

- The following conflict solution strategies may be distinguished by means of the questionnaire: problem analysis, cognitive restructuring, adaptation (conformism), acting on emotional impetus, seeking emotional balance, withdrawal and asking for help.

Survey of temperament and character:
The Hungarian version of Cloninger's Temperament and Character Inventory adapted by Rózsa at al. [1, 2] was filled in by the respondents. The main scales of the measure describe four temperament and three character dimensions:

- The temperament-scales are: novelty seeking, harm avoidance, reward dependence, persistence.
- The character-scales are: self-directedness, cooperativeness, self-transcendence.

3. RESULTS

Temperament and Character Type Distribution

When elaborating temperament and character types Cloninger took the medians while Rózsa et al. took the T value of 50 as basis [2].

For a more pronounced representation and partitioning of temperament and character types we departed from the mentioned methods of sorting. In our research the emphasis was laid on quartiles and those points were considered as low values, which fell in the first quartile of a particular quartile, and those were taken into account as high values which fell in the fourth quartile (table 1).

Table 1. Quartiles of the Temperament and Character Inventory

Scales of the Temperament and Character Inventory	Median value	Quartiles			
		first	second	third	fourth
Novelty Seeking	22	0-18	19-22	23-26.5	27-40
Harm Avoidance	17	0-12	13-17	18-22	23-35
Reward Dependence	18	0-15	16-18	19-20	21-24
Persistence	4	0-2	3-4	5-6	7-8
Self-Directedness	28	0-24	25-28	29-33.5	34-44
Cooperativness	30	0-25	26-30	31-35	36-42
Self-Transcendence	17	0-13	14-17	18-21	22-33

Table 2 represents Cloninger's classification of temperament types as well as their distribution within the sample.

**Table 2. Aspects of classification and distribution
of temperament types in the sample**

Temperament types	Novelty Seeking	Harm Avoidance	Reward Dependence	Cases	Contibutional rate (%)	Women	Men
Antisocial	high	low	low	50	7,3	25	25
Histrionic	high	low	high	48	7	32	16
Passive-aggressive	high	high	high	27	4	23	4
Borderline	high	high	low	23	3,4	14	9
Obsessive-compulsive	low	high	low	51	7,5	30	21
Schizoid	low	low	low	27	4	10	17
Cyclothimic	low	low	high	33	4,8	27	6
Passive-dependent	low	high	high	53	7,8	49	4

Taking the foregoing aspects into consideration we managed to classify 312 persons (210 females, 102 males) as per the temperament types.

Rózsa et al. [2] found the rate of occurrence of individual temperament types to be between 8% and 15% in the normative/standard sample. In our case this value varied between 3.4% and 7.8% in the inspected sample. This deviation is attributable to the sterner method of categorisation applied by us.

The highest rate of occurrence was found by us in the case of passive-dependent (7.8%), obsessive-compulsive (7.5%) and antisocial (7.3%) temperaments. The lowest occurrence rate was revealed in the case of borderline (3.3%), passive-aggressive (4%) and schizoid (4%) temperaments. These results, apart from schizoid temperament, correspond to the findings of Rózsa et al. on the normative/standard sample.

Table 3 illustrates Cloninger's classification of character types, as well as their distribution within the sample.

Table 3. Aspects of character-type classification and their distribution in the sample

Character types	Self-Directedness	Cooperativeness	Self-Transcendence	Cases	Contributional rate (%)	Women	Men
Irritable	low	high	low	24	3.5	21	3
Melancholic	low	low	low	79	11.6	51	28
Authoritier	high	low	low	27	4	16	11
Ordered	high	high	low	63	9.2	44	19
Cyclothimic	low	high	high	44	6.5	29	15
Schizotipic	low	low	high	48	7	26	22
Paranoid	high	low	high	16	2.3	12	4
Creative	high	high	high	61	9	51	10

With regard to the foregoing criteria we managed to classify 362 persons (250 females, 112 males) as per the character types.

The occurrence rate of different character types ranged between 2.3% and 11.6%. The highest occurrence rate was shown by melancholic (11.6%), ordered (9.2%) and creative (9%), while the lowest rate of occurrence was shown by paranoid (2.3%), irritable (3.5%) and authoriter (4%) types.

Depressive Syndromes Typical to Respective Temperament and Character Types

We examined what interrelation might exist between temperament and character types and depressive syndromes (table 4).

Table 4. Interrelations of temperament and character types with depressive syndromes

	Probability for exceeding (p<)												
	1	2	3	4	5	6	7	8	9	10	11	12	13
Antisocial temperament	0.007*	0.013*	n.s.	0.028*	n.s.	n.s.	n.s.	n.s.	0.048*	n.s.	n.s.	n.s.	n.s.
Histrionic temperament	n.s.	0.005*	n.s.	n.s.	n.s.	n.s.	n.s.	n.s.	n.s.	n.s.	n.s.	n.s.	n.s.
Passive-aggressive temperament	n.s.	0.000	n.s.	n.s.	n.s.	0.009	0.021	n.s.	n.s.	n.s.	n.s.	0.004	n.s.
Borderline temperament	n.s.	n.s.	0.000	n.s.	0.005	n.s.	n.s.	n.s.	n.s.	n.s.	0.012	n.s.	n.s.
Obsessive-compulsive temperament	0.000	0.000	0.000	0.038	0.001	n.s.	n.s.	0.001	0.033	n.s.	n.s.	n.s.	0.035
Schizoid temperament	n.s.	n.s.	n.s.	n.s.	n.s.	n.s.	n.s.	n.s.	n.s.	0.011*	0.008*	n.s.	n.s.
Cyclothimic temperament	0.024*	n.s.	0.044*	0.000*	0.001*	0.008*	n.s.	n.s.	0.000*	n.s.	0.009*	0.004*	n.s.
Passive-dependent temperament	n.s.	0.000	0.046	n.s.	n.s.	n.s.	n.s.	n.s.	n.s.	0.008	n.s.	n.s.	n.s.
Irritable character	n.s.	0.029	n.s.	n.s.	n.s.	n.s.	n.s.	n.s.	n.s.	0.027	n.s.	n.s.	n.s.
Melancholic character	0.000	0.000	0.000	0.000	0.000	0.006	n.s.	0.001	0.019	n.s.	0.000	0.012	0.030
Authorier character	n.s.	0.004*	n.s.	n.s.	n.s.	n.s.	n.s.	n.s.	n.s.	n.s.	0.031*	0.047*	n.s.
Ordered character	0.000*	0.002*	0.000*	0.005*	0.002*	0.048*	0.014*	0.015*	0.007*	0.019*	0.000*	0.036*	n.s.
Cyclothimic character	0.000	0.006	0.007	n.s.	0.000	0.003	n.s.	n.s.	0.000	0.000	0.049	0.004	0.039
Schizotipic character	n.s.	0.035	0.012	n.s.	0.028	n.s.	0.018	n.s.	0.045	0.004	0.037	0.048	n.s.

Table 4. (Continued)

Probability for exceeding (p<)	1	2	3	4	5	6	7	8	9	10	11	12	13
Paranoid character	n.s.	n.s.	n.s.	n.s.	n.s.	n.s.	n.s.	n.s.	n.s.	n.s.	n.s.	n.s.	n.s.
Creative character	0.003*	0.032*	0.001*	0.005*	0.000*	0.040*	0.002*	0.021*	0.001*	0.013*	n.s.	n.s.	n.s.

1=Sadness, 2= Pessimism, 3= Sense of failure, 4=Dissatisfaction, 5= Guilt, 6= Fear of punishment, 7=Suicide thoughts, 8= Indecisiveness, 9= Social withdrawal, 10= Self-image change, 11= Work difficulty, 12= Fatigability, 13= Anorexia, n.s. =not significant, *= negative correlation.

In comparison with the sample as a whole we found the following syndromes typical to individual temperament types:

- *Antisocial temperament* was not significantly more characterised by sadness, pessimism and inability of decision making than the rest of the sample.
- *Histrionic temperament* was revealed to be characterised with a low-level pessimism.
- We managed to indicate that *passive-aggressive temperament* was characterised by pessimism, fear of punishment, suicide thoughts and fatigability.
- *We found that borderline temperament* was characterised by defeats, guilt and work difficulty.
- *Obsessive-compulsive temperament* was found to be characterised by sadness, pessimism, dissatisfaction, sense of failure, the feeling of guilt, inability of decision making and the anorexia.
- *Schizoid temperament* was found to be characterised self-image change and work difficulty.
- *Cyclothimic temperament* was characterised by sadness, dissatisfaction, sense of failure, the feeling of guilt, fear of punishment, inability of decision making, work difficulty and fatigability.
- In the case of *passive-dependent temperament* we managed to indicate pessimism, sense of failure and self-image change.

In comparison with the sample as a whole we found the following syndromes typical to individual character types:

- *Irritable character* was characterised by pessimism and self-image change
- In the case of *melancholic character* sadness, pessimism, dissatisfaction, sense of failure, the feeling of guilt, fear of punishment, indecisiveness, the inability of decision making, fatigability, work difficulty and anorexia were found to be typical.
- *Authoriter character* was found to be characterised by pessimism, work difficulty and the lack of fatigue.
- *Ordered character* was found to be least characterised by depressive syndromes, and except for the lack of appetite every syndrome was significantly less typical of it than of the rest of the sample.
- *Cychlothimic character* was found to be characterised by sadness, pessimism, defeats, the feeling of worthlessness, disposition to fear of punishment, inability of decision making, bodily image disorder, work-incapability, fatigue and anorexia.
- We managed to indicate that *schizotipic character* was featured by pessimism, sense of failure, the feeling of guilt, suicide thoughts, inability of decision making, self-image change, work difficulty and fatigability.
- *Paranoid character* showed significant interrelationship with none of the depressive syndromes
- In the case of *creative character* we also found no typical depressive syndromes, and except for work- difficulty, fatigability and anorexia, every syndrome was significantly less typical of this character than of the rest of the sample.

Dysfunctional Attitudes Typical to Respective Temperament and Character Types

In table 5 it is demonstrated what correlations are showed by individual temperament and character types with the individual scales of Dysfunctional Attitude Scale.

Table 5. Correlations between different temperament and character types with the scales of Dysfunctional Attitude Scale

	Probability for exceeding (p<)						
	1	2	3	4	5	6	7
Antisocial temperament	0,000*	0,013*	0,029*	n.s.	n.s.	n.s.	n.s.
Histrionic temperament	n.s.	n.s.	n.s.	0,021*	n.s.	n.s.	n.s.
Passive-aggressive temperament	n.s.	0,034	n.s.	n.s.	n.s.	n.s.	0,010
Borderline temperament	n.s.	n.s.	n.s.	n.s.	n.s.	n.s.	0,017
Obsessive-compulsive temperament	n.s.	n.s.	0,002	n.s.	n.s.	n.s.	0,033
Schizoid temperament	n.s.	n.s.	n.s.	n.s.	0,001*	n.s.	n.s.
Cyclothimic temperament	n.s.	n.s.	n.s.	n.s.	n.s.	n.s.	0,001*
Passive-dependent temperament	n.s.	0,035					0,007
Irritable character	n.s.	n.s.	n.s.	n.s.	n.s.	n.s.	n.s.
Melancholic character	n.s.	n.s.	n.s.	0,036	n.s.	n.s.	0,033
Authoriter character	n.s.	n.s.	n.s.	n.s.	n.s.	n.s.	n.s.
Ordered character	0,009*	0,017*	0,020*	0,002*	n.s.	n.s.	0,000*
Cychlothimic character	n.s.	n.s.	n.s.	n.s.	n.s.	n.s.	n.s.
Schizotipic character	0,000	n.s.	0,003	n.s.	n.s.	n.s.	0,000
Paranoid character	n.s.	n.s.	n.s.	n.s.	n.s.	0,033	n.s.
Creative character	n.s.	n.s.	n.s.	0,029*	n.s.	n.s.	0,021*

1= Demand for external recognition, 2= Demand for affections, 3= Performance demand, 4= Perfectionism, 5= Expectations towards environment, 6= Altruism, 7= External control, n.s.= not significant, *= negative correlation.

In comparison with the sample as a whole we found the following constellations to be typical to individual temperament types:

- *Antisocial temperament* was typically characterised by low demand for external recognition, demand for affection and performance demand.
- In the case of *histrionic temperament* we found only low perfectionism typical.
- *Passive-aggressive temperament* was characterised by increased external control and demand for affection.
- In the case of *borderline temperament* we found only intensified external control typical.
- *Obsessive-compulsive temperament* was only characterised by high performance demand, and intensive external control.
- *Schizoid temperament* was typically characterised by a low level of expectations towards environment.
- *Cyclothimic temperament* was primarily characterised by the endeavour to autonomy.
- We found that *passive-dependent temperament* was characterised by external control and an increased demand for affections.

In comparison with the sample as a whole we found the following constellations to be typical to individual character types:

- We found no typical attitude with respect to *irritable character.*
- *Melancholic character* was characterised by perfectionism and external control.
- In the case of *authoriter character* we have not found any typical attitude either.
- *Ordered character* seemed to long less for external recognition, but the demand for performance and affection, as well as an intensified endeavour to autonomy were observable in this case.
- We found no typical attitude in the case of *cyclothimic character*
- In the case of the *schyzotipic character* we found higher demand for external recognition and performance, as well as higher rate of external control typical.
- *Paranoid character* was significantly different from the specimen as a whole regarding intensified altruism.
- We found that *creative character* was less characterised by perfectionism, but an intensified endeavour to autonomy was detectable in this case.

Coping Strategies Typical to Respective Temperament and Character Types

Table 6 illustrates what correlations we have found between temperament and character types and the scales of the Conflict Solving Questionnaire.

Table 6. Correlations between temperament and character types with the scales of Conflict Solving Questionnaire

	Probability for exceeding (p<)						
	1	2	3	4	5	6	7
Antisocial temperament	n.s.	n.s.	n.s.	n.s.	0.037*	n.s.	0.000*
Histrionic temperament	n.s.	0.026	0.034	n.s.	n.s.	0.002	0.006
Passive-aggressive temperament	n.s.	n.s.	n.s.	0.044	n.s.	n.s.	0.016
Borderline temperament	0.000*	n.s.	n.s.	0.014	n.s.	0.007	0.050*
Obsessive-compulsive temperament	n.s.	n.s.	n.s.	n.s.	0.034	n.s.	n.s.
Schizoid temperament	n.s.	n.s.	n.s.	0.003*	n.s.	n.s.	n.s.
Cyclothimic temperament	n.s.	0.004	n.s.	0.004*	n.s.	n.s.	0.008
Passive-dependent temperament	n.s.	n.s.	0.045*	n.s.	n.s.	0.003*	0.024
Irritable character	n.s.	0.004*	n.s.	n.s.	n.s.	0.034*	n.s.
Melancholic character	0.000*	0.000*	n.s.	n.s.	n.s.	n.s.	0.005*
Authoriter character	n.s.	n.s.	0.050*	n.s.	0.016*	n.s.	0.017*
Ordered character	0.002	n.s.	n.s.	0.000*	0.028*	0.001*	n.s.
Cychlothimic character	n.s.	n.s.	0.009	n.s.	0.000	n.s.	0.000
Schizotipic character	0.027*	n.s.	n.s.	0.000	0.025	0.004	n.s.
Paranoid character	n.s.	n.s.	n.s.	n.s.	0.033	n.s.	n.s.
Creative character	n.s.	0.005	n.s.	0.014*	n.s.	n.s.	0.000

1= Problem analysis, 2=Cognitive restructuring, 3=Conformance, 4=Emotion driven actions, 5=Retrieval, 6=Seeking emotional balance ,7= Call for assistance, n.s.=not significant, *=negative correlation.

In comparison with the sample as a whole we found the following coping modes to be typical to individual temperament types:

- We found that *antisocial temperament* is significantly less predisposed to retrieval and call for assistance.
- We managed to reveal that *histrionic temperament* was regarding emotion driven strategies characterised by an intensified endeavour to achieve emotional balance. When examining the problem focused strategies we revealed the preference of cognitive restructuring and conformance. The application of the call for assistance as a coping strategy was also typical to this temperament type.

- From among emotion-driven strategies we found that *passive-aggressive temperament* was characterised by emotion-driven actions. Additionally, in this case we managed to indicate a higher level of the call for assistance.
- From among problem-focused strategies we indicated a low level of problem analysis in the case of *borderline temperament*. We found the preference of emotion-driven actions from among emotion driven coping strategies, and the endeavour to achieve emotional balance typical to this temperament type. In hard situations however this temperament type is less prone to call for assistance from the environment.
- When examining the problem-focused strategies we found no typical coping strategy in the case of *obsessive-compulsive temperament*, and even in the case of emotion-driven strategies we could only detect an increased disposition to retrieval.
- We found no typical problem-focused strategy to *schizoid temperament*. From among emotion driven strategies a lower degree of emotion-driven actions was found to be typical of this temperament type.
- We found the preference of cognitive restructuring typical to *cyclothimic temperament* in the field of problem-focused coping. In the case of emotion driven strategies only a low level of emotion-driven actions was revealed. Furthermore we found that such a temperament is more predisposed to call for assistance than the rest of the sample.
- In the case of *passive-dependent temperament* a lower level of conformance and seeking emotional balance, and a higher level of disposition to call for assistance were found to be typical.

In comparison with the sample as a whole we found the following coping modes to be typical to individual character types:

- To *irritable character* in the field of problem-focused coping cognitive restructuring, while from among emotion-driven strategies a lower level of seeking emotional balance was found to be typical.
- In the case of *melancholic character* problem analysis and cognitive restructuring as well as a low level of call for assistance were indicated to be typical.
- In the case of *authoriter character* we found conformance and retrieval, as well as the lack of call for assistance typical.
- In the field of problem focused coping we found predisposition to problem analysis typical to *ordered character*. When examining the emotion focused strategies we managed to indicate emotion driven actions, a retrieval and a low level of emotional balance seeking.
- We found that *cyclothimic character* was characterised by conformance, retrieval and a high level of call for assistance.
- In the case of *schizotipic character* when examining the problem-focused coping we found a low disposition to problem analysing typical. When examining the emotional focused strategies emotion-driven actions, retrieval and a higher level of emotional balance seeking were revealed.
- We found only preference of retrieval typical to *paranoid character*.

- In the case of *creative character* we managed to indicate the preference of cognitive restructuring, a low level of emotion driven actions, as well as the predisposition to the call for assistance.

4. DISCUSSION

Drawing the conclusion from the findings of our research we revealed that the following depressive syndromes, dysfunctional attitudes and coping strategies were typical to individual temperament types:

- The *antisocial temperament* is less dependent on environment, and less requires the external recognition and affection. Such a personality has a lower demand for performance. A person with this temperament type is cheerful, hopeful and determined in general. This temperament requests the environment for no assistance even in difficult situations or circumstances and is less apt to retrieval.
- The *histrionic temperament* is not characterised by perfectionism. Problem resolution is featured by cognitive restructuring and conformance. This temperament is able to request assistance in hard situations, and takes efforts to restore the emotional balance. Pessimism is not typical of this personality.
- *Passive-aggressive temperament* is externally controlled, with increased need of loving. This personality is prone to become hopeless easily, which may be accompanied by the endeavour to self-punishment and the occurrence of suicide thoughts. This temperament is susceptible to fatigue. In difficult situations this temperament is disposed to emotion induced actions, and requests the environment for assistance for the resolution of problems.
- The *borderline temperament* feels worthless, and defeat-burdened, for which – due to the fact that such temperament has external control – the environment is held responsible. In difficult situations no analysis of problems is typical of such a personality, more rather emotion induced actions or the quest for emotional balance is characterising this temperament. The feeling of being incapable of work may also characterise this personality.
- *Obsessive-compulsive temperament* is characterised by a high demand for performance coupled with external control. This feature as well as the inability of decision making however renders more difficulty to the achievement of the performance level conforming to the expectations of such personality, which, coupled with the feeling of failure, may bring forth a persistent feeling of dissatisfaction, hopelessness, sadness and worthlessness. In hard situations this character is prone to retrieval. Loss of appetite may also be typical of such a personality.
- The *schizoid temperament* has a good load bearing capability, with good work-ability and self-acceptance. This temperament has less expectation towards the environment, and controls the emotions appropriately, consequently in difficult situations of life such a temperament is not characterised by emotion induced actions.

- The *cyclothimic temperament,* as per the outcome of our research, endeavours intensively to the achievement of autonomy, and resolves problems with cognitive restructuring. In difficult situations this personality asks the environment for assistance, keeps the emotions under control, and no emotion induced actions are typical of this temperament. In general this person is cheerful, satisfied and determined, with highly estimated personality, who is energetic and has good load bearing abilities.
- The *passive-dependent temperament* has external control, and turns to the environment with an increased level of demand for affection. This personality becomes hopeless easily, is sensitive to defeat and has a low level of self-acceptance. In difficult situations this person requests the environment for assistance, but it takes less effort to adaptation and to the quest of emotional balance. Owing to the dependence on external control this person expects the resolution of problems primarily from the environment.

The following depressive syndromes, dysfunctional attitudes and coping strategies were found to be typical of individual character types:

- In difficult situations *irritable character* is not characterised by the application of cognitive restructuring and the quest for emotional balance. This personality is apt to become hopeless easily and shows a low level of self-acceptance.
- The *melancholic character* is typically perfectionist. Despite the lack of ability to cognitive restructuring, the disability to decision making, as well as of external control, however the lack of requesting the environment for assistance thwarts the efforts for perfectionism, which may lead to the occurrence of failure, sadness, hopelessness, dissatisfaction, the feeling of worthlessness, disposition to self-punishment, disinterest, fatigue, disability to work and the occurrence of the lack of appetite.
- The *authoriter character* does not adapt itself to the environment in difficult circumstances, does not request the environment for assistance, and is not disposed to retrieval. This person is optimistic, energetic and able to work.
- The *ordered character* does not expect external recognition and affections from the environment, and is characterised by the endeavour to increased autonomy. This personality demands performance intensively. In difficult situations this character is disposed to act upon emotions, but is not prone to retrieval, or the quest for emotional balance, but this person faces dilemmas and is apt to the analysis of problems. This character is emotionally balanced, has a high self-esteem, energetic and has high load bearing ability.
- We found that the *cyclothimic character* is featured by sadness, hopelessness, failure, the feeling of worthlessness, disposition to self-punishment, disability to decision making, bodily image disorder, disability to work, fatigue and the lack of appetite. In difficult situations this person is able to ask the environment for assistance, takes efforts to adaptation and retrieval.
- The *schizotipic character* has high demands for external recognition and performance coupled with the need for external control. However the disability to decision making and the lack of aptness to problem analysis makes the realisation of

performance demands more difficult. This character is sensitive to failure, which may cause hopelessness, the feeling of worthlessness, and the occurrence of suicide thoughts. This character is dissatisfied with him or herself, cannot bear strains and is susceptible to fatigue. In difficult situations such a person is disposed to act upon emotions, the quest for emotional balance or retrieval.

- The *paranoid character* is characterised by altruistic attitudes. In difficult situations this personality is apt to retrieval. This showed no significant correlation with any of the depressive syndromes.

- The *creative character* is characterised by the intensive endeavours to autonomy. No perfectionism features this personality. In difficult situations this character requests the environment for assistance, and is not disposed to emotion induced actions, or the quest for emotional balance, or retrieval, but the problems are resolved by way of cognitive restructuring instead. This character is emotionally balanced and shows high self-esteem.

REFERENCES

[1]   Cloninger C. R., & Bayon C., & Svrakic D. M. (1998). Measurement of temperament and charachter in mood disorders: a model of fundamental states as personality types. *Journal of Affective Disorders, 51,* 21-32.

[2]   Rózsa S., & Kállai, J., & Osváth, A., & Bánki M. Cs. (2005). Temperamentum és karakter: Cloninger pszichobiológiai modellje. A Cloninger-féle temperamentum és karakter kérdőív felhasználói kézikönyve. [Temperament and character. Cloninger's psychobiologycal model. The handbook of the Cloninger Temperament and Character Inventory.] Budapest: Medicina Könyvkiadó Rt.

[3]   Beck, A.T., & Beck R.W. (1972). Screening depressed patients in family practice. A rapid technique. *Postgraduate Medicine, 52,* 81-85.

[4]   Margitics, F. (2005). Prediszponáló tényezők kapcsolata a szubklinikus depressziós tünetegyüttessel főiskolai hallgatóknál. [Interrelation between predisposition factors and sub clinical depression syndrome at college students.] *Psychiatria Hungarica, 20,* 211-223.

[5]   Kopp, M. (1994). *Orvosi pszichológia. [Medical psychology.]* Budapest: SOTE Magatartástudományi Intézet.

[6]   Weisman, A.N., & Beck, A.T. (1979). *The Dysfunctional Attitude Scale.* Thesis, University of Pennsylvania.

[7]   Folkmann, S., & Lazarus, R.S. (1980). An analysis of coping in a middle-aged community sample. *Journal of Health and Social Behaviour, 21,* 219-239.

Chapter 7

SUBJECTIVE WELL-BEING AND INDIVIDUAL ASPIRATIONS OF COLLEGE STUDENTS

ABSTRACT

In the course of our research we examined the level of subjective well-being among college students, and what individual aspirations they had. There were 545 women and 167 men students (n=712) involved in the research. In terms of the indicators of subjective well-being, students scored the highest values in self-evaluation, followed by positive attitude to life and pleasures of life. The low values measured on the depressive scale suggest the lack of depressive moods. No considerable difference between the two genders was measured at subjective well-being. The only exemption to that was observed in somatic symptoms and reactions, as women were found to be more susceptible to such reactions than men. When examining the importance of individual aspirations, we recorded the highest points at health, personal progress and social connections. Most participants in the survey found these personal aspirations very imporant. The college students involved in the project ascribed the lowest importance to the three extrinsic aspirations: fame, wealth and image. Intrinsic aspirations were therefore favoured by college students over the extrinsic ones. If priorities are examined in a breakdown according to genders, intrinsic aspirations were found more important by both sexes, with slight differences in emphasis. In terms of the probability of various types of aspiration, the highest scores were also measured at intrinsic aspirations. In that case, the order of priority was social relations, personal progress and health. It was followed by social commitment and, finally, extrinsic aspirations, in the order of image, wealth and fame. When the order of probability is examined in a breakdown according to genders, women fully comply with the general trend, whereas in the case of the men there is a slight deviation at one point only, they tend to place wealth before image. In terms of the implementation of the types of aspiration, the tendency is similar, as we find the highest points at the intrinsic ones, in the following order: social relations, health and personal progress. Here an extrinsic aspiration, image wedged in, followed by social commitment, wealth and fame. The order was the same in both genders.

1. INTRODUCTION

The concept of subjective well-being is extremely complex, and the approaches various experts use are also varied. Diener arranges the recent approaches into three groups [1]:

- The first type of theories contains those that follow the footsteps of antique thinkers, philosophers and regard subjective well-being as the possession of positive characteristic features and/or emotions that are based upon the fulfilment and activation of personal ambitions and will lead to self-expression and self-implementation.
- The second category contains the so-called top-down models, emphasizing the role of personality and the interpretation of life experience in the definition of subjective well-being. In these theories subjective well-being is identified with satisfaction with life, which is based upon subjective value judgments and is closely related to the evaluative and attributive functions of the personality.
- The third group of theories is the one that includes the subjective, bottom-up approaches. These theories consider subjective well-being as the summary of pleasure experienced by the person concerned. An individual is happy after, and as a result of, gathering a large number of positive emotions, moods and happy moments.

Today it is obvious that it is necessary to integrate the various theories, as any one of the approaches above in itself will not be suitable for the interpretation of the complex issue of subjective well-being.

According to recent research, it is possible to describe subjective well-being with three major factors [1]:

- A level of satisfaction with life as a whole, referring to a cognitive judgment system, with which the individual evaluates his/her life in an overall way.
- Frequency and intensity of positive emotions/affectivity – pleasure and happiness.
- The relative scarcity of negative emotions, depression, fear, anxiety, sadness and other negative situations.

The fact that the individual factors – pleasant emotions, satisfaction with life, negative emotions – are separate and independent of each other, has been justified by several surveys [2].

Although formerly it was believed that positive and negative emotions were located on the opposing ends of the same axis, today it is regarded as proven that the levels of positive and negative emotions within one individual are relatively independent of each other. There is evidence suggesting that separate neurological operations are responsible for pleasant and unpleasant emotions [3].

Diener [3] asserts that subjective well-being has several clearly discernible components: satisfaction with life, satisfaction with various parts of life, e. g. job, marriage, the high levels of positive emotions (pleasant experiences and moods) and the low level of negative emotions (unpleasant experiences and moods).

Initial research projects into subjective well-being examined the connections between personality and happiness, seeking an answer to questions as to whether long-lasting happiness as a feature of the personality exists, or whether there are personal characteristic features that are closely related to happiness. Several research programmes suggest that certain characteristic features such as extraversion show a positive correlation with well-being [4] whereas neuroticism has a negative effect on personal happiness [5]. Personal characteristic features, however, only explain approximately 30% of the variance [6], so the question is still open as to what other specific factors are responsible for subjective well-being.

New tendencies in psychology, emerging in the late eighties and early nineties offered new possibilities for measuring subjective well-being and subjective satisfaction with life. The new psychological approaches tend to place more emphasis on personal endeavours [7] personal objectives [8] and individual aspirations and strivings [9, 10].

These new research trends draw inspiration from the work of humanistic theoreticians like Rogers, Maslow and Fromm, who believe that our decisions regarding important things in life, what we do in order to achieve our objectives and how we utilize our internal potentials are the decisive factors in our personal subjective well-being. We believe that our life is sensible and valuable if and when our objectives are congruent with our internal selves, and we are committed to reach our goals, thus improving our personality.

In Emmons's theory [7] personality is interpreted as a motivation system, in which the emphasis is on the personal objectives (or system of objectives) that drive human behaviour and on the achievement of the objectives.

The research conducted by Emmons and Diener [11] suggest that individuals who regard their own actions as ones that do not generate conflicts tend to be more satisfied with life. Diener and Fujita [12] in another examination that they carried out in order to study the interrelations of personal goals, social and internal resources and well-being/satisfaction with life found that social and internal resources have a considerable effect on satisfaction with life. Non-social external resources (e. g. material goods, money) do not appear to influence emotional well-being, but they correlate with satisfaction with life to a medium extent. Furthermore, an examination of the individual patterns of various resources revealed differences between men and women. Women find social objectives such as emotional control and social skills, including the resources required for achieving these goals, more important than men do. The system of objectives of men, on the other hand, largely contains performance objectives like authority, achievements in sports and knowledge acquired through experience. The resources leading to these goals are primarily performance and instrumental means.

Kasser and Ryan [9], when examining the connections between values, objectives and subjective well-being, found that individuals giving priority to extrinsic goals (their endeavours are focused on financial success, the acquisition of material goods) demonstrated a generally lower well-being and a worse psychological situation, regardless of their gender, than those for whom intrinsic goals (self-acceptance, social relations and social commitments) were more important.

The research programmes conducted by Kasser and Ryan [10] as well as other researchers among people of various age and social backgrounds (lower, middle and upper classes) in cultures different from that in the U.S., suggest that there is a reverse proportion between the attribution of great importance to material values and subjective well-being. The studies mentioned above justify the theories of humanistic thinkers that for subjective well-being intrinsic objectives are more central than extrinsic ones.

Personal strivings, as dynamic characteristics of the personality, may function as important indicators of subjective well-being. In the course of our research we intended to reveal the level of subjective well-being of college students, what individual aspirations they had, and what connections existed between individual aspirations and subjective well-being.

We also intended to find any difference, if such existed, between the two genders in this respect.

Our initial research hypotheses were the following:

1. There are no differences in the level of subjective well-being between the two genders [2, 13].
2. For college students (in accordance with the representative samples from Hungary), intrinsic objectives, particularly health, personal advancement and social relations are the most important [14].
3. In terms of personal aspirations, there will considerable differences between the two genders, with women attributing greater significance to the intrinsic aspirations and image, while men regarding wealth more important [14].
4. As for intrinsic aspirations, women will find health and social relations the most important, while men tend to ascribe the greatest importance to personal advancement [14].

2. METHOD

Participants

Data was collected among students at the College of Nyíregyháza. We collected data randomly at every faculty and participation was voluntary and it was done with their consent. 700 students took part in the research and 681 of them provided valuable data (465 women and 216 men).

The average age was 19.98 (standard deviation 1.51) the median value was 20 years.

When forming the test groups, we used the scores achieved on the Combined Intrinsic and Extrinsic Aspirations Indicators scale of the Aspiration Inventory as a guideline. Students were arranged into the quarters of the sample according to their scores on the scale (table 1).

Students scoring low on the scale were arranged into the first quarter of the sample, whereas students scoring the highest on the scale were placed in the fourth quarter.

**Table 1. The quartiles of scores on aggregate chart scales
of intrinsic and extrinsic aspirations**

	Quartiles	
	first	third
Intrinsic Aspirations: importance	114	130
Intrinsic Aspirations: probability	94	115
Intrinsic Aspirations: realization	74	100
Extrinsic Aspirations: importance	52	72
Extrinsic Aspirations: probability	46	66
Extrinsic Aspirations: realization	36	56

At the examination of the importance of intrinsic aspirations, 180 students were in the group representing the lowest scores, and 189 students belonged to the group with the high scores.

At the examination of the probability of intrinsic aspirations, 172 students were in the group representing the lowest scores, and 180 students belonged to the group with the high scores.

At the examination of the realization of intrinsic aspirations, 177 students were in the group representing the lowest scores, and 175 students belonged to the group with the high scores.

At the examination of the importance of extrinsic aspirations, 177 students were in the group representing the lowest scores, and 189 students belonged to the group with the high scores.

At the examination of the probability of extrinsic aspirations, 175 students were in the group representing the lowest scores, and 169 students belonged to the group with the high scores.

At the examination of the realization of extrinsic aspirations, 177 students were in the group representing the lowest scores, and 171 students belonged to the group with the high scores.

Measures

The following research methods were used:
Examination of subjective well-being
Diener's Life Satisfaction Scale [3].

Diener [3] asserts that subjective well-being is an indicator of how individuals evaluate their lives from cognitive and affective aspects. Individuals make judgments about their lives as a whole and about various parts of the whole, e. g. work, family, marriage, etc. In this way, subjective well-being has several components independent of each other. The scale measures the cognitive factor and global satisfaction with life with the help of five statements. Respondents marked the validity of the statements for their particular life on a seven-grade Likert-scale.

The Hungarian version of the scale was successfully used by Martos et al. [15] in their research programme. They found the reliability of the scale excellent (Cronbach-alpha=0,890).

Bern Subjective Well-Being Inventory [16].

Grob [17] describes two dimensions of subjective well-being: satisfaction and "ill existence." The four components of satisfaction are: a positive attitude to life, a positive self-esteem, the lack of depressive mood and pleasures in life. Positive attitude towards life means, on the one hand, that the individual has a generally positive approach to life and, on the other hand, that the person is convinced that he or she lives a meaningful life. Depressive mood means the lack of energy, sadness and withdrawal. The lack of depressive mood is an important indicator of subjective well-being, of satisfaction with life. Pleasures in life mean a positive evaluation and appreciation of human existence, as well as the acceptance of one's personal abilities and characteristics. The two components of "ill existence" are personal problems on the one hand and the somatic symptoms and reactions on the other. Personal problems include to what extent a person is preoccupied and annoyed by various problems. Personal problems also include how the individual recognizes and accepts the problems that crop up in their direct social environment as well as how sensitive the individual is to the problematic situations. Somatic symptoms and reactions mean the ability of the individual to convert his or her inner tensions into somatic symptoms.

The questionnaire developed by Grob contains the following dimensions:

- A positive attitude towards life
- Personal problems
- Somatic symptoms and reactions
- Self-esteem
- Depressive mood
- Pleasure in life

Respondents are requested to mark on a seven-grade Likert scale to what extent a statement applies to them.

The Hungarian adaptation of the questionnaire was done by Sallay [17], who found the reliability of the scales good (Cronbach-alpha=0.69-0.81).

Survey of the individual aspirations

Aspiration Inventory [11].

The self-determination theory of Deci and Ryan [18, 19] constitutes the theoretical foundation of the questionnaire, according to which the sound functioning, growth and inner integration of a personality is primarily driven by the efforts to satisfy certain innate and universal needs. The authors identify three of these needs as elementary: the individual's desire for autonomy, the individual's desire for positive relations and an ability for competent, independent action. These basic needs serve as the major motivation forces of the personality. It is possible to satisfy these needs through self-motivation (intrinsic motives) and external motivation (extrinsic motives). The authors revealed the most characteristic intrinsic and extrinsic motives through empirical research. The motives were formulated in the form of aspirations, objectives in life.

The Aspiration Inventory [10] is a means of revealing long term objectives and aspirations; it contains a total of 35 aspirations (objective, motive), clustered around 7 categories of goals in life, represented by the 7 scales of the questionnaire. 5 items belong to each of the 7 scales. These are the following:

- Wealth
- Reputation
- Image (good appearance)
- Growth (personal anvancement)
- Social relations (good personal connections)
- Society (social commitment)
- Health

Respondents are supposed to judge the aspirations listed in the questionnaire according to three aspects on a seven-grade Likert-scale:

- Importance (How important is the objective to you?)
- Probability (What is the likelihood of this happening to you in the future?)
- Realization (How much of the objective above have you been able to achieve?)

The most important extrinsic motivations (aspirations): wealth, reputation and image. The primary intrinsic motivations (aspirations): personal advancement, social relations and social commitment. Kasser and Ryan [10] assert that health does not clearly belong to any of the aspirations. In compliance with the findings of several international research programmes, V. Komlósi et al. [14], as a result of a survey in Hungary, listed health with the intrinsic aspirations

In the course of the Hungarian adaptation of the questionnaire, V. Komlósi et al. [14] found the reliability of the dimensions excellent (Cronbach-alpha=0.72-0.91).

3. RESULTS

Descriptive and Comparative Statistics

The descriptive and comparative statistics of the findings achieved with Diener's Life Satisfaction Scale and the Bern Subjective Well-being Inventory are provided (for the whole of the sample and in a breakdown according to the two genders) in table 2. In order to make the figures comparative, the average values and dispersions are set to one answer on the scale.

Table 2. The descriptive and comparative statistics of Diener's Life Satisfaction Scale and the Bern Subjective Well-being Inventory

	Total (n=712)		Women (n=545)		Men (n=167)	
	Mean Value	Standard Deviation	Mean Value	Standard Deviation	Mean Value	Standard Deviation
Diener's Satisfaction with Life Scale	4.38	1.22	4.40	1.20	4.34	1.28
Bern Subjective Well-Being Questionnaire: Positive attitude towards life	3.46	0.65	3.46	0.64	3.47	0.67
Bern Subjective Well-Being Questionnaire: Személyes problémák	2.75	0.85	2.77	0.9	2.67	0.70
Bern Subjective Well-Being Questionnaire: somatic symptoms and reactions	2.15***	0.75	2.21	0.75	1.96	0.71
Bern Subjective Well-Being Questionnaire: Self-esteem	4.45	0.87	4.45	0.85	4.47	0.92
Bern Subjective Well-Being Questionnaire: Depressive mood	2.16	0.70	2.14	0.68	2.24	0.74
Bern Subjective Well-Being Questionnaire: Pleasure of life	3.46	0.66	3.46	0.64	3.42	0.74

*p<0,05; **p<0,01; ***p<0,001.

When examining university students' satisfaction with life, Diener et al. [2] measured an average of 4.7 (dispersion=1.28). In our college students we found a value somewhat lower than that; our findings approximately match a medium value on Likert's scale.

Out of Grob's satisfaction index, students scored the highest values at self-esteem, followed by positive attitude towards life and pleasures of life, with almost the same figures. The low scores on the scale of depressive mood is an indicator of the lack of depressive mood.

The indicators of Grob's "ill existence" were low, with the indicators of personal problems somewhat higher than those of somatic rections. These values–as matched to Likert's five-grade scale–suggest a high level of self-esteem, a somewhat above-the-average level of the positive attitude to life and pleasures of life, an average level of personal problems, and levels below the average at somatic symptoms and depressive mood. Sallay [17] conducted a survey among adolescents, and found similar values, except at self-esteem (average=1,96, dispersion=0,67), where their figure was lower and at depressive mood (average=3,68, dispersion=0,71) where their figure was higher. These differences are explained by the changes of the adolescent age, and in the sample we examined was not characterized by these deviations.

A comparative statistical analysis of the two genders shows any considerable difference between men and women in the somatic symptoms and reactions only. Women appear to be more susceptible to such reactions than men ($t=3.944$, $p<0.005$).

The descriptive and comparative statistics of Aspiration Inventory are summarized in table 3.

In the whole sample, when the importance of the various aspirations was examined, the highest values were measured at health, personal advancement and social relations. Most respondents found these aspirations extremely important, which is also indicated by the fcat the dispersion was the smallest at health and social relations (the large standard deviation found at personal growth, on the other hand, indicates the large personal differences at this point). The least important goals in life for the respondents were the three extrinsic aspirations, reputation, wealth and image. Intrinsic aspirations are therefore favoured by college students over the extrinsic ones. These findings largely coincide with the results obtained by V. Komlósi et al. [14] as a result of their examination conducted on a representative sample (with the exception of the value of standard deviation found at personal growth, which was larger in their sample). Szondy [13] also found intrinsic aspirations more characteristic in his sample of late adolescent age (average age: 17.38 years). The order of importance of the aspirations was the following: social relations, health, personal growth, followed by social responsibility. The adolescents also listed extrinsic aspirations with the least important ones, in the order of wealth, image and finally reputation.

Table 3. The descriptive and comparative statistics of Aspiration Inventory

	Total (n=712)		Women (n=545)		Men (n=167)	
	Mean Value	Standard Deviation	Mean Value	Mean Value	Standard Deviation	Mean Value
Wealth: importance	22.8	5.6	23.6	5.7	24,1	5.4
Wealth: probability	19.9	5.1	19.8	5	20,3	5.5
Wealth: realization	15.1	5.5	15	5.4	15,2	5.9
Reputation: importance	17**	7.3	16.6	7.2	18,4	7.4
Reputation: probability	14.9***	5.9	14.5	5.7	16,4	6.3
Reputation: realization	11.5***	5	11.1	4.7	12,9	5.7
Image: importance	23***	6.7	23.8	6.6	20.6	6.7
Image: probability	21.1***	5.9	21.7	5.8	19.3	6.1
Image: realization	19.4*	6.3	19.7	6.2	18.3	6.5
Personal advancement: importance	32.3	13.2	32.1	8.4	32.6	22.8
Personal advancement: probability	26.8*	4.7	27.1	4.5	26	5
Personal advancement: realization	21.8	5.5	22	5.5	21.1	5.6
Personal relationships: importance	32***	3.2	32.3	2.8	30.1	4.4
Personal relationships: probability	28.5***	4.7	29	4.2	26.8	5.8
Personal relationships: realization	24.5***	9.4	25.7	9.4	22.6	7.2
Social commitment: importance	25.6*	5.8	25.9	5.6	24.5	6.4
Social commitment: probability	22.3**	5.7	22.7	5.6	21	5.9
Social commitment: realization	16.7	6.1	17	6	16.1	6.1
Health: importance	32.3***	3.4	32.7	2.9	31	4.5
Health: probability	26.1***	5.5	26.6	5.3	24.5	6.1
Health: realization	23.5*	6.5	23.8	6.4	22.4	6.8
Intrinsic: importance	121.5***	11.7	122.8	10.3	117.3	14.8
Intrinsic: probability	103.7***	16.1	105.2	14.9	98.8	18.6
Intrinsic: realization	86.9**	19.7	88.1	19.2	82.9	20.1
Extrinsic: importance	64.7	17.1	64.6	17.2	65.1	16.9
Extrinsic: probability	56.6	14.2	56.6	14	56.4	14.8
Extrinsic: realization	46.2	14.2	46.1	13.8	46.7	15.5

*$p<0,05$; **$p<0,01$; ***$p<0,001$.

If we examine the order of importance, we find the intrinsic aspirations on the top of the lists for both genders, with smaller shifts in emphasis. While the order of importance for women is health, social relations and personal advancement, men place personal advancement in the first position, followed by health and social relations. Social commitment is the fourth in the list of both genders. On the list of women it is followed by image and wealth, with approximately the same values, whereas wealth precedes image on the list of men. Reputation is the last on the lists of both sexes. Our findings in connection with the extrinsic aspirations match those of V. Komlósi et al. [14] obtained from their survey of a representative sample. They found health as the most important intrinsic aspiration in both genders, followed by social relations on the list of women, and personal growth on the list of men. The comparative statistical analysis (two paired t-test) suggests that women scored considerably higher in the combined index of intrinsic aspirations, health, social relations, image and social commitment. Men, on the other hand, gave higher points to reputation. Szondy [13] also observed this difference between the two sexes, except the higher value of reputation on the list of men. No considerable difference was observed between the two genders in the combined index of extrinsic aspirations, personal growth and wealth. These findings only partially match the results obtained by V. Komlósi et al. [14] from their representative sample. In their findings, men scored significantly higher in their aspiration for wealth, whereas women scored considerably higher in image, personal advancement, social relations, social commitment and health than men did.

An examination of the entire sample from the aspect of the probability of the various aspirations, the highest values were also measured at the intrinsic aspirations, in the order of social relations, personal advancement and health. They are followed by the extrinsic aspirations, in the order of the image, wealth and reputation. Szondy [13] found the same order late adolescent age. An examination of the order or probability according to the two genders, we find the same tendency in women. In men, there is only one deviation, as they place wealth before image. At the probability of various aspirations, we found similar differences to those observed at the degree of importance. The only exception was that women gave considerably greater emphasis to personal advancement.

When analysing the realization of the aspirations in the whole sample, the highest values are observed at the intrinsic aspirations. The order is the following: social relations, health and personal growth. The fourth one here an extrinsic aspiration, image, followed by social commitment, wealth and reputation. This was the order in both genders. In connection with realization, Szondy [13] found a similar pattern among adolescents, with slight changes of emphasis: health, social relations, personal advancement, image, social responsibility, wealth and reputation. At the probability of various aspirations, we found similar differences in those observed at the degree of importance. The only exception to that was that no significant difference between the two genders was observable in terms of the realization of social commitment.

Unfortunately, we did not have an opportunity to compare the probability and realization of the various aspirations with the representative sample, as V. Komlósi et al. [14] did not provide relevant data in their study.

4. Discussion

In the course of our reseach, we examined subjective well-being and personal aspirations in a sample of college students.

In subjective well-being–in acordance with our initial hypothesis–we did not observe any considearable difference. The only exceptions to that were identified in somatic symptoms and reactions, as women were found to be more susceptible to these reactions than men. These results are in full harmony with the findings of other research programmes [2, 13].

In our second hypothesis, the prevalence of individual aspirations, we had assumed that– similar to the results of the research of V. Komlósi et al. [14] conducted on a representative Hungarian sample–college students would find intrinsic objectives, and within those, health, personal relations and social relations the most important. Our research findings suggest that college students also tend to favour intrinsic aspirations over the extrinsic aspirations. In compliance with the findings of V. Komlósi at al. [14], college students found health, personal growth and social relations the most important personal aspirations. They found the extrinsic aspirations, reputation, wealth and image as the least important objectives in life.

We have also been able to confirm our third initial hypothesis, that is, there would be a considerable difference between the genders in terms of individual aspirations, as women would find image, whereas men would find wealth as important goals in life, as suggested by the findings of V. Komlósi et al. [14] earlier. In the sample of college students, however, men–unlike earlier findings with Hungarian samples–gave priority to reputation over wealth, which is different from the list of importance set up by women.

In research conducted in Hungary by V. Komlósi et al. [14], it was found that women put social relations directly after health on the list of intrinsic aspirations, whereas for men the most important ambition was personal growth. Our fourth hypothesis was that it was going to be the same with college students. We found the domination of intrinsic aspirations in both genders, with only slight shifts of emphasis. For women health, social relations and personal growth was the order, for men personal advancement was on the top of the list, followed by health and social relations. These results are in full compliance with the results of V. Komlósi et al. [14].

REFERENCES

[1]   Urbán, R. (1995). Boldogság, személyiség és egészség. [Happiness, personality and health.] *Magyar Pszichológiai Szemle, 35*, 379-404.

[2]   Diener, E., & Such, E.M., & Lucas, R.E., & Smith, H.L. (1999). Subjective well-being: three decades of progress. *Psychology Bulletin, 125, 276-302.*

[3]   Diener, E. (2000). Subjective well-being: the science of happiness and a proposal for a national index. *American Psychologist, 55*, 34-43.

[4]   Lu, L., & Shih, J.B. (1997). Personality and happiness: is mental health a mediator? *Personality and Individual Differences, 22*, 249-256.

[5]   Brebner, J., & Donaldson, J., & Kirby, N., & Ward, L. (1995). Relationship between happiness and personality. *Personality and Individual Differences, 19*, 251-258.

[6]   Chan, R., & Joseph, S. (2000). Dimensions of personality, domains of aspirations, and subjective well-being. *Personality and Individual Differences, 28*, 347-354.

[7]   Emmons, R. A. (1986). Personal strivings: an approach to personality and subjective well-being. *Journal of Personality and Social Psychology, 51*, 1058-1068.

[8] Brunstein, J.C. (1993). Personal goals and subjective well-being: a longitudinal study. *Journal of Personality and Social Psychology, 65,* 1061-1070.

[9] Kasser, T., & Ryan, R.M. (1993). A dark side of the American dream: correlates of financial success as a central life aspiration. *Journal of Personality and Social Psychology, 65,* 410-422.

[10] Kasser, T., & Ryan, R.M. (1996), Further examining the American dream: differential correlates of intrinsic and extrinsic goals. *Personality and Social Psychology Bulletin, 22,* 280-287.

[11] Emmons, R.A., & Diener, E. (1985): Personality correlates of subjective well-being. *Personality and Social Psychology Bulletin, 11,* 89-97.

[12] Diener, E., & Fujita (1995). Recources, personal strivings, and subjective well-being: a nomothetic and idiographic approach. *Journal of Personality and Social Psychology, 68,* 926-935.

[13] Szondy, M. (2004). A szubjektív jóllét és a törekvések kapcsolata késői serdülőkorban. [Interrelation between subjective well-being and aspirations at late adolescent.] *Alkalmazott Pszichológia, 4,* 53-72.

[14] V. Komlósi, A., & Rózsa S., & Bérdi M., & Móricz É., & Horváth D. (2006). Az Aspirációs Index hazai alkalmazásával szerzett tapasztalatok. [Experiences obtained with the domestic application of the Aspiration Index.] *Magyar Pszichológiai Szemle, 61,* 237-250.

[15] Martos, T., & Szabó G., & Rózsa S. (2006). Az Aspirációs Index rövidített változatának pszichometriai jellemzői hazai mintán. [Psychometric characteristics of the abridged Aspiration Index with domestic sample.] *Mentálhigiéné és Pszichoszomatika, 7,* 171-191.

[16] Grob, A. (1995). Subjective well-being and significant life-events across the life-span. *Swiss Journal of Psychology, 54,* 3-18.

[17] Sallay, H. (2004): Entering the job market: belief in a just world, fairness and well-being of graduation students. In C. Dalbert, & H. Sallay (Eds.), *The Justice Motive in Adolescence and Young Adulthood: Origins and Consequences* (pp. 215-231). Routledge, London: Routledge.

[18] Deci, E. L., & Ryan, R. M. (1985). *Intrinsic Motivation and Self-determination in Human Behavior.* New York: Plenum.

[19] Deci, E. L., & Ryan, R. M. (2000). The "what" and "why" of goal pursuits: human needs and the self-determination of behaviour. *Psychological Inquiry, 11,* 227-268.

ABOUT THE AUTHORS

Dr. Ferenc Margitics PhD. Associate Professor, the leader of Health Psychology group. E-mail: margif@nyf.hu

Zsuzsa Pauwlik PhD Student, Assistant Professor, member of Health Psychology group. E-mail: pauwlik@nyf.hu

INDEX